100 BEST
Holiday
COOKIES

Publications International, Ltd.
Favorite Brand Name Recipes at www.fbnr.com

Recipe development on pages 40, 44, 48, 54, 56, 64, 70, 76, 90, 92, 96, 102, 104, 106, 114, 132, 134, 138, 144 and 150 by Bev Bennet.

Photography on pages 5 top left, 9, 17, 25, 27, 35 top left, 41, 45, 49, 57, 59, 65 top left, 71, 77, 81, 91, 93, 97, 99, 103, 105, 107, 113, 115, 125 bottom left, 133, 139, 145 and 151 by Chris Cassidy Photography, Inc.

Photography on front cover and page 55 by Proffitt Photography Ltd., Chicago.

Pictured on the front cover: Chunky Nut Blondie Drops *(page 54)*.

Pictured on the back cover *(clockwise from top left):* Little Christmas Puddings *(page 80),* Ice Skates *(page 72),* Truffle Brownie Bites *(page 150)* and Chewy Peanut Butter Brownies *(page 110).*

ISBN-13: 978-1-4127-2546-0
ISBN-10: 1-4127-2546-1

Library of Congress Control Number: 2007920132

Manufactured in China.

8 7 6 5 4 3 2 1

Microwave Cooking: Microwave ovens vary in wattage. Use the cooking times as guidelines and check for doneness before adding more time.

Preparation/Cooking Times: Preparation times are based on the approximate amount of time required to assemble the recipe before cooking, baking, chilling or serving. These times include preparation steps such as measuring, chopping and mixing. The fact that some preparations and cooking can be done simultaneously is taken into account. Preparation of optional ingredients and serving suggestions is not included.

Contents

Old-Fashioned Favorites

Golden Kolacky

½ cup (1 stick) butter, softened
4 ounces cream cheese, softened
1 cup all-purpose flour
Fruit preserves

1. Beat butter and cream cheese in large bowl until smooth. Gradually add flour to butter mixture, blending until mixture forms soft dough. Divide dough in half; wrap each half in plastic wrap. Refrigerate about 1 hour or until firm.

2. Preheat oven to 375°F. Roll out dough, one half at a time, on floured surface to ⅛-inch thickness. Cut into 2½-inch squares. Spoon 1 teaspoon preserves into center of each square. Bring up two opposite corners to center; pinch together tightly to seal. Fold sealed tip to one side; press to seal. Place 1 inch apart on ungreased cookie sheets. Bake 10 to 15 minutes or until lightly browned. Remove to wire racks; cool completely.

Makes about 2½ dozen cookies

*Clockwise from top left: Golden Kolacky,
Buttery Almond Cutouts (page 28),
Banana Crescents (page 13) and
Pumpkin White Chocolate Drops (page 18)*

Molasses Spice Cookies

1 cup granulated sugar
¾ cup shortening
¼ cup molasses
1 egg
2 cups all-purpose flour
2 teaspoons baking soda
1 teaspoon ground ginger
1 teaspoon ground cinnamon
1 teaspoon ground cloves
¼ teaspoon salt
¼ teaspoon dry mustard
½ cup granulated brown sugar* or granulated sugar

Granulated brown sugar is brown sugar that has been processed to have a light, dry texture that is similar to regular granulated sugar. It can be found in the baking aisles of most supermarkets.

1. Preheat oven to 375°F. Grease cookie sheets.

2. Beat granulated sugar and shortening about 5 minutes in large bowl until light and fluffy. Add molasses and egg; beat until fluffy.

3. Combine flour, baking soda, ginger, cinnamon, cloves, salt and mustard in medium bowl. Add to shortening mixture; beat just until blended.

4. Place granulated brown sugar in shallow dish. Shape dough into 1-inch balls; roll in sugar to coat. Place 2 inches apart on prepared cookie sheets. Bake 15 minutes or until lightly browned. Let cookies stand on cookie sheets 2 minutes. Remove cookies to wire racks; cool completely.

Makes about 6 dozen cookies

Santa's Chocolate Cookies

1 cup (2 sticks) butter
⅔ cup semisweet chocolate chips
¾ cup sugar
1 egg
½ teaspoon vanilla
2 cups all-purpose flour
   Melted semisweet chocolate, toasted coconut and sliced almonds
   (optional)

1. Combine butter and chocolate chips in large microwavable bowl. Microwave on HIGH 30 seconds; stir. Repeat as necessary until chips are melted and mixture is smooth. Let cool slightly. Add sugar, egg and vanilla; stir until well blended. Add flour; stir until well blended. Cover; refrigerate 30 minutes or until firm.

2. Preheat oven to 350°F. Shape dough by tablespoonfuls into balls; place 1 inch apart on ungreased cookie sheets.

3. Bake 8 to 10 minutes or until set. Remove to wire racks to cool completely. Decorate as desired with melted chocolate, toasted coconut and almonds.   *Makes about 3 dozen cookies*

Helpful Hint

Home-baked cookies make great inexpensive gifts for friends and family. Place them in a paper-lined tin or on a decorative plate; cover with plastic wrap and tie with a colorful ribbon. For a special touch, include the recipe.

Santa's Chocolate Cookies

Holiday Sugar Cookies

1 cup (2 sticks) butter, softened
¾ cup sugar
1 egg
2 cups all-purpose flour
1 teaspoon baking powder
¼ teaspoon salt
¼ teaspoon ground cinnamon
    Colored sugar or sprinkles (optional)

1. Beat butter and sugar in large bowl with electric mixer at medium speed until creamy. Add egg; beat until fluffy.

2. Stir in flour, baking powder, salt and cinnamon until well blended. Form dough into ball; wrap in plastic wrap and flatten. Refrigerate about 2 hours or until firm.

3. Preheat oven to 350°F. Roll out a small portion of dough to ¼-inch thickness on lightly floured surface with lightly floured rolling pin. (Keep remaining dough wrapped in refrigerator.)

4. Cut dough with 3-inch cookie cutters. Decorate cutouts with colored sugar; place on ungreased cookie sheets. Repeat with remaining dough.

5. Bake 7 to 9 minutes until edges are lightly browned. Let cookies stand on cookie sheets 1 minute; transfer to wire racks to cool completely.

Makes about 3 dozen cookies

Holiday Sugar Cookies

Pebbernodders

3 cups all-purpose flour
1 teaspoon *each* baking powder and ground cinnamon
½ teaspoon *each* ground ginger and ground cloves
1½ cups (3 sticks) butter, softened
1½ cups sugar
3 eggs
2 teaspoons freshly grated lemon peel

1. Mix flour, baking powder, cinnamon, ginger and cloves in medium bowl. Beat butter and sugar in large bowl until creamy. Add eggs and lemon peel; beat until well blended. Gradually add flour mixture; mix just until blended.

2. Grease cookie sheets. Divide dough into four equal pieces; shape each piece into ¾-inch-thick rope about 12 inches long. Place ropes on prepared cookie sheets. Freeze about 30 minutes or until firm.

3. Preheat oven to 375°F. Cut frozen ropes into ¼-inch-thick slices; place 1 inch apart on greased cookie sheets. Bake 10 minutes or until lightly browned. Cool completely.   *Makes about 16 dozen small cookies*

Mini Chip Snowball Cookies

1½ cups (3 sticks) butter or margarine, softened
¾ cup powdered sugar
1 tablespoon vanilla extract
½ teaspoon salt
3 cups all-purpose flour
2 cups (12-ounce package) NESTLÉ® TOLL HOUSE® Semi-Sweet
    Chocolate Mini Morsels
½ cup finely chopped nuts
    Powdered sugar

PREHEAT oven to 375°F.

BEAT butter, sugar, vanilla extract and salt in large mixer bowl until creamy. Gradually beat in flour; stir in morsels and nuts. Shape level tablespoons of dough into 1¼-inch balls. Place on ungreased baking sheets.

BAKE for 10 to 12 minutes or until cookies are set and lightly browned. Remove from oven. Sift powdered sugar over hot cookies on baking sheets. Cool on baking sheets for 10 minutes; remove to wire racks to cool completely. Sprinkle with additional powdered sugar, if desired. Store in airtight containers.   *Makes about 5 dozen cookies*

Banana Crescents

½ cup chopped almonds, toasted
6 tablespoons sugar, divided
½ cup margarine, cut into pieces
1½ cups plus 2 tablespoons all-purpose flour
⅛ teaspoon salt
1 extra-ripe, medium DOLE® Banana, peeled
2 to 3 ounces semisweet chocolate chips

• Pulverize almonds with 2 tablespoons sugar in blender.

• Beat margarine, almond mixture, remaining 4 tablespoons sugar, flour and salt until well blended.

• Purée banana in blender; add to almond mixture and mix until well blended.

• Shape tablespoonfuls of dough into logs, then shape into crescents. Place on ungreased cookie sheet. Bake at 375°F for 25 minutes or until golden. Cool on wire rack.

• Melt chocolate in microwavable dish at MEDIUM (50% power) 1½ to 2 minutes, stirring once. Dip ends of cookies in chocolate. Refrigerate until chocolate is set.   *Makes about 2 dozen cookies*

Helpful Hint

Toasting nuts intensifies their flavor and crunch. To toast nuts, spread them on a baking sheet and place in a preheated 350°F oven for 8 to 10 minutes. Always cool nuts to room temperature before combining them with other ingredients.

Gingerbread People

½ cup (1 stick) butter, softened
½ cup packed brown sugar
⅓ cup water
⅓ cup molasses
 1 egg
 4 cups all-purpose flour
 2 teaspoons baking soda
 1 teaspoon ground ginger
½ teaspoon ground allspice
½ teaspoon ground cinnamon
½ teaspoon ground cloves
    Assorted icing and candies

1. Beat butter and brown sugar in large bowl with electric mixer at medium speed until creamy. Add water, molasses and egg; beat until blended. Add flour, baking soda, ginger, allspice, cinnamon and cloves; beat until well blended. Wrap dough tightly with plastic wrap; refrigerate about 2 hours or until firm.

2. Preheat oven to 350°F. Grease cookie sheets. Roll out dough on lightly floured surface with lightly floured rolling pin to ⅛-inch thickness. Cut with cookie cutter. Place cutouts 2 inches apart on prepared cookie sheets.

3. Bake 12 to 15 minutes or until set. Cool 1 minute on cookie sheets. Remove to wire racks to cool completely. Decorate as desired.

Makes about 4½ dozen cookies

Gingerbread People

Chocolate-Frosted Lebkuchen

4 eggs
1 cup sugar
1½ cups all-purpose flour
1 cup (6 ounces) ground almonds*
⅓ cup candied lemon peel, finely chopped
⅓ cup candied orange peel, finely chopped
1½ teaspoons ground cinnamon
1 teaspoon freshly grated lemon peel
½ teaspoon ground cardamom
½ teaspoon ground nutmeg
¼ teaspoon ground cloves
3 squares (1 ounce each) semisweet chocolate, coarsely chopped
1 tablespoon butter

*To grind almonds, place in food processor or blender. Process until thoroughly ground to a dry, not pasty, texture.

1. Beat eggs and sugar in large bowl with electric mixer at high speed 10 minutes.

2. Meanwhile, combine flour, almonds, candied lemon and orange peels, cinnamon, grated lemon peel, cardamom, nutmeg and cloves in another large bowl. Add egg mixture; stir until well blended. Cover; refrigerate 12 hours or overnight.

3. Preheat oven to 350°F. Line cookie sheets with parchment paper or grease and dust with flour. Drop dough by rounded teaspoonfuls 2 inches apart onto prepared cookie sheets. Bake 8 to 10 minutes or just until browned. *Do not overbake.* Remove to wire racks to cool slightly.

4. Meanwhile, combine chocolate and butter in small microwavable bowl. Microwave on HIGH 30 seconds; stir. Repeat as necessary until chocolate is melted and mixture is smooth. Spread over tops of warm cookies. Let stand until glaze is set. *Makes about 5 dozen cookies*

Chocolate-Frosted Lebkuchen

Pumpkin White Chocolate Drops

2 cups (4 sticks) butter, softened
2 cups granulated sugar
1 can (about 16 ounces) solid-pack pumpkin
2 eggs
4 cups all-purpose flour
2 teaspoons pumpkin pie spice*
1 teaspoon baking powder
½ teaspoon baking soda
1 package (12 ounces) white chocolate chips
1 container (16 ounces) cream cheese frosting
¼ cup packed brown sugar

Substitute 1 teaspoon ground cinnamon, ½ teaspoon ground ginger and ¼ teaspoon each ground allspice and ground nutmeg for 2 teaspoons pumpkin pie spice.

1. Preheat oven to 375°F. Grease cookie sheets.

2. Beat butter and granulated sugar in large bowl with electric mixer at medium speed until light and fluffy. Add pumpkin and eggs; beat until well blended. Add flour, pumpkin pie spice, baking powder and baking soda; beat just until blended. Stir in white chocolate chips.

3. Drop dough by teaspoonfuls about 2 inches apart onto prepared cookie sheets. Bake 16 minutes or until set and lightly browned. Cool 1 minute on cookie sheets. Remove to wire racks to cool completely.

4. Combine frosting and brown sugar in small bowl. Spread on warm cookies.   *Makes about 6 dozen cookies*

Danish Lemon-Filled Spice Cookies

2¼ cups all-purpose flour
1 teaspoon ground cinnamon
½ teaspoon ground ginger
½ teaspoon ground allspice
½ teaspoon ground nutmeg
¼ teaspoon salt
¾ cup (1½ sticks) butter, softened
¾ cup sugar
¼ cup milk
1 egg yolk
1 teaspoon vanilla
Additional sugar
Lemon Filling (recipe follows)

1. Combine flour, cinnamon, ginger, allspice, nutmeg and salt in medium bowl. Beat butter, sugar, milk, egg yolk and vanilla in large bowl with electric mixer at medium speed until light and fluffy. Gradually add flour mixture, beating at low speed until dough forms. Cover dough and refrigerate 30 minutes or until firm.

2. Preheat oven to 350°F. Grease cookie sheets. Shape teaspoonfuls of dough into ½-inch balls; place 2 inches apart on prepared cookie sheets. Flatten each ball to ¼-inch thickness with bottom of glass dipped in sugar. Pierce top of each cookie decoratively with fork. Bake 10 to 13 minutes or until golden brown. Remove cookies to wire racks; cool completely.

3. Prepare Lemon Filling. Spread filling on flat sides of half of cookies. Top with remaining cookies, pressing flat sides together. Let stand at room temperature until set.   *Makes about 3 dozen sandwich cookies*

Lemon Filling: Combine 2¼ cups sifted powdered sugar, 3 tablespoons lemon juice, 1½ tablespoons softened butter and ½ teaspoon lemon extract in medium bowl; beat with electric mixer at medium speed until smooth.

Rum Fruitcake Cookies

1 cup sugar
¾ cup shortening
3 eggs
⅓ cup orange juice
1 tablespoon rum extract
3 cups all-purpose flour
2 teaspoons baking powder
1 teaspoon baking soda
1 teaspoon salt
2 cups (8 ounces) chopped candied mixed fruit
1 cup raisins
1 cup nuts, coarsely chopped

1. Preheat oven to 375°F. Lightly grease cookie sheets. Beat sugar and shortening in large bowl until fluffy. Add eggs, orange juice and extract; beat 2 minutes.

2. Combine flour, baking powder, baking soda and salt in medium bowl. Add candied fruit, raisins and nuts. Stir into shortening mixture.

3. Drop dough by rounded teaspoonfuls 2 inches apart onto prepared cookie sheets.

4. Bake 10 to 12 minutes or until golden brown. Let stand on cookie sheets 2 minutes. Remove to wire racks; cool completely.

Makes about 6 dozen cookies

Rum Fruitcake Cookies

Butter Cookies

¾ cup (1½ sticks) butter, softened
¼ cup granulated sugar
¼ cup packed light brown sugar
1 egg yolk
1¾ cups all-purpose flour
¾ teaspoon baking powder
⅛ teaspoon salt

1. Beat butter, sugars and egg yolk in medium bowl until well blended. Add flour, baking powder and salt; mix well. Cover; refrigerate until firm, about 4 hours or overnight.

2. Preheat oven to 350°F. Roll dough on lightly floured surface with lightly floured rolling pin to ¼-inch thickness; cut into desired shapes with cookie cutters. Place on ungreased cookie sheets.

3. Bake 8 to 10 minutes or until edges begin to brown. Remove to wire racks; cool completely. *Makes about 2 dozen cookies*

Chocolate Rum Balls

½ cup (1 stick) butter, softened
⅓ cup granulated sugar
1 egg yolk
1 tablespoon dark rum
1 teaspoon vanilla
1 cup all-purpose flour
¼ cup unsweetened cocoa powder
1 cup finely chopped walnuts or pecans
Powdered sugar

1. Beat butter, granulated sugar and egg yolk in large bowl until light and fluffy. Blend in rum and vanilla. Stir in flour and cocoa. Stir in nuts. Cover; refrigerate until firm, about 1 hour.

2. Preheat oven to 350°F. Lightly grease cookie sheets or line with parchment paper. Shape dough into 1-inch balls; place 2 inches apart on prepared cookie sheets. Bake 15 to 20 minutes or until firm. Remove to wire racks to cool. Roll in powdered sugar. *Makes about 3 dozen cookies*

Cherry Walnut Tassies

½ cup (1 stick) butter, softened
1 package (3 ounces) cream cheese, softened
1 cup cake flour
2 egg yolks
¾ cup packed light brown sugar
1 teaspoon vanilla
⅛ teaspoon salt
½ cup finely chopped dried cherries
½ cup finely chopped walnuts

1. Beat butter and cream cheese in large bowl with electric mixer at medium speed until blended. Stir in flour just until stiff dough forms. Wrap in plastic wrap; refrigerate at least 1 hour.

2. Preheat oven to 325°F. Divide dough into 24 pieces. Press each piece firmly onto bottom and up side of ungreased mini (1¾-inch) muffin cup.

3. Beat egg yolks, brown sugar, vanilla and salt just until smooth. Stir in cherries and walnuts. Divide evenly among muffin cups.

4. Bake 30 to 35 minutes or until pastry is golden brown and filling is set. Cool completely in pans on wire racks.   *Makes 2 dozen cookies*

 ## Helpful Hint

Brown sugar is a mixture of granulated sugar and molasses that adds a rich flavor to baked goods. When fresh, it is moist and clingy, however, it can easily dry out. Add a slice of apple or bread to the box or bag to help retain moisture.

Finnish Nut Logs

1 cup (2 sticks) butter, softened
½ cup plus ⅓ cup sugar, divided
3 eggs
½ teaspoon ground cardamom
½ teaspoon almond extract
2¼ to 2½ cups all-purpose flour
1 cup finely chopped almonds

1. Beat butter and ½ cup sugar in large bowl with electric mixer at medium speed until light and fluffy. Beat in 1 egg, cardamom and almond extract until well blended. Gradually add 1½ cups flour, beating at low speed until well blended. Stir in enough remaining flour with spoon to form soft dough. Form dough into disc; wrap in plastic wrap and refrigerate until firm, at least 30 minutes or overnight.

2. Grease cookie sheets. Divide dough into 8 equal pieces. With floured hands, shape each piece into ½-inch-thick rope about 12 inches long. Cut ropes into 2-inch logs; place on prepared cookie sheets. Refrigerate 30 minutes.

3. Preheat oven to 350°F. Combine almonds and remaining ⅓ cup sugar in medium bowl. Beat remaining 2 eggs with fork in shallow dish until foamy; dip logs into beaten egg mixture. Roll in nut mixture to coat; return to cookie sheets.

4. Bake 15 minutes or until lightly browned. Remove cookies to wire racks; cool completely. *Makes about 4 dozen cookies*

Mini Pecan Tarts

Tart Shells
   2 cups all-purpose flour
   1 teaspoon granulated sugar
   Pinch salt
   ¾ cup (1½ sticks) cold butter, cut into pieces
   ⅓ cup ice water

Filling
   1 cup powdered sugar
   ½ cup (1 stick) butter
   ⅓ cup dark corn syrup
   1 cup chopped pecans
   36 pecan halves

1. For tart shells, combine flour, granulated sugar and salt in large bowl. Using pastry blender or two knives, cut in cold ¾ cup butter until mixture resembles coarse crumbs. Add water, 1 tablespoon at a time, kneading mixture until dough forms a ball. Wrap dough in plastic wrap; refrigerate at least 30 minutes.

2. Preheat oven to 375°F. Grease 36 mini (1¾-inch) muffin cups. Roll out dough on lightly floured surface to ⅛-inch thickness. Cut dough with 2½-inch round cookie cutter; press rounds into prepared muffin cups. Bake about 8 minutes or until very lightly browned. Remove from oven. *Reduce oven temperature to 350°F.*

3. For filling, combine powdered sugar, ½ cup butter and corn syrup in 2-quart saucepan. Cook over medium heat, stirring occasionally, until mixture comes to a full boil, 4 to 5 minutes. Remove from heat; stir in chopped pecans. Spoon into warm baked shells. Top each with pecan half. Bake 5 minutes. Cool completely; remove from pans.

Makes 3 dozen tarts

Mini Pecan Tarts

Buttery Almond Cutouts

1½ cups granulated sugar
1 cup (2 sticks) butter, softened
¾ cup sour cream
2 eggs
3 teaspoons almond extract, divided
1 teaspoon vanilla
4⅓ cups all-purpose flour
1 teaspoon baking powder
1 teaspoon baking soda
½ teaspoon salt
2 cups powdered sugar
2 tablespoons milk
1 tablespoon light corn syrup
Assorted food coloring and decors

1. Beat granulated sugar and butter in large bowl until light and fluffy. Add sour cream, eggs, 2 teaspoons almond extract and vanilla; beat until smooth. Add flour, baking powder, baking soda and salt; beat until well blended. Divide dough into 4 pieces; flatten each piece into disc. Wrap each disc tightly with plastic wrap. Refrigerate at least 3 hours or up to 3 days.

2. Preheat oven to 375°F. Working with one disc of dough at a time, roll out on floured surface to ¼-inch thickness. Cut dough into desired shapes using 2½-inch cookie cutters. Place cutouts about 2 inches apart on ungreased cookie sheets. Bake 7 to 8 minutes or until edges are firm and lightly browned. Transfer to wire racks to cool completely.

3. Combine powdered sugar, milk, corn syrup and remaining 1 teaspoon almond extract in small bowl; stir until smooth. Divide glaze among 3 or 4 small bowls; tint with desired food coloring. Frost and decorate cookies as desired; let stand until set.   *Makes about 3 dozen cookies*

Spiced Raisin Cookies with White Chocolate Drizzle

2 cups all-purpose flour
1½ teaspoons ground cinnamon
1 teaspoon baking soda
1 teaspoon ground ginger
½ teaspoon ground allspice
¼ teaspoon salt
1 cup sugar
¾ cup butter, softened
¼ cup molasses
1 egg
1 cup SUN-MAID® Raisins or Golden Raisins
4 ounces white chocolate, coarsely chopped

HEAT oven to 375°F.

COMBINE flour, cinnamon, baking soda, ginger, allspice and salt in a small bowl. Set aside.

BEAT sugar and butter until light and fluffy.

ADD molasses and egg; beat well.

BEAT in raisins. Gradually beat in flour mixture on low speed just until incorporated.

DROP dough by tablespoonfuls onto ungreased cookie sheets 2 inches apart. Flatten dough slightly.

BAKE 12 to 14 minutes or until set. Cool on cookie sheets 1 minute; transfer to wire racks and cool completely.

MICROWAVE chocolate in heavy, resealable plastic bag at high power 30 seconds. Turn bag over; heat additional 30 to 45 seconds or until almost melted. Knead bag with hands to melt remaining chocolate. Cut ⅛-inch corner off one end of bag. Drizzle cooled cookies with chocolate. Let stand until chocolate is set, about 20 minutes.   *Makes about 2 dozen cookies*

Prep Time: 15 minutes
Bake Time: 14 minutes

Date Pinwheel Cookies

1¼ cups dates, pitted and finely chopped
¾ cup orange juice
½ cup granulated sugar
1 tablespoon butter
3 cups plus 1 tablespoon all-purpose flour, divided
2 teaspoons vanilla, divided
1 cup packed brown sugar
4 ounces cream cheese, softened
¼ cup shortening
2 eggs
1 teaspoon baking soda
½ teaspoon salt

1. Combine dates, orange juice, granulated sugar, butter and 1 tablespoon flour in medium saucepan over medium heat. Cook 10 minutes or until thick, stirring frequently. Remove from heat. Stir in 1 teaspoon vanilla; set aside to cool.

2. Beat brown sugar, cream cheese and shortening in large bowl with electric mixer at medium speed about 3 minutes or until creamy. Add eggs and remaining 1 teaspoon vanilla; beat 2 minutes.

3. Combine remaining 3 cups flour, baking soda and salt in medium bowl. Add to shortening mixture; stir just until blended. Divide dough in half. Roll one half of dough on lightly floured surface into 12×9-inch rectangle. Spread half of date mixture evenly over dough, leaving ¼-inch border at top short edge. Starting at opposite end, tightly roll up dough jelly-roll style. Wrap in plastic wrap; freeze at least 1 hour. Repeat with remaining dough and date mixture.

4. Preheat oven to 350°F. Grease cookie sheets. Using heavy thread or dental floss, cut dough into ¼-inch slices. Place slices 1 inch apart on prepared cookie sheets.

5. Bake 12 minutes or until lightly browned. Let cookies stand on cookie sheets 2 minutes. Remove to wire racks to cool completely.

Makes 6 dozen cookies

Date Pinwheel Cookies

Peanut Butter Cut-Outs

½ **cup creamy peanut butter**
6 **tablespoons margarine or butter, softened**
½ **cup packed brown sugar**
⅓ **cup KARO® Light or Dark Corn Syrup**
1 **egg**
2 **cups flour**
1½ **teaspoons baking powder**
1 **teaspoon ground cinnamon (optional)**
⅛ **teaspoon salt**

1. In large bowl with electric mixer at medium speed, beat peanut butter, margarine, brown sugar, corn syrup and egg until smooth. Reduce speed; beat in 1 cup flour, baking powder, cinnamon and salt. With spoon, stir in remaining 1 cup flour.

2. Divide dough in half. Between two sheets of waxed paper on large cookie sheets, roll each half of dough ¼ inch thick. Refrigerate until firm, about 1 hour.

3. Preheat oven to 350°F. Remove top piece of waxed paper. With floured cookie cutters, cut dough into shapes. Place on ungreased cookie sheets.

4. Bake 10 minutes or until lightly browned. Do not overbake. Let stand on cookie sheets 2 minutes. Remove from cookie sheets; cool completely on wire racks. Reroll dough trimmings and cut additional cookies. Decorate as desired. *Makes about 5 dozen cookies*

Prep Time: 20 minutes, plus chilling and decorating
Bake Time: 10 minutes, plus cooling

Tip: Use scraps of dough to create details on cookies.

Peanut Butter Cut-Outs

Christmas Cookie Quickies

Chocolate Spritz

    2 squares (1 ounce each) unsweetened chocolate
    1 cup (2 sticks) butter, softened
    ½ cup granulated sugar
    1 egg
    1 teaspoon vanilla
    ¼ teaspoon salt
    2¼ cups all-purpose flour
      Cocoa powder or powdered sugar

1. Preheat oven to 400°F. Line cookie sheets with parchment paper. Melt chocolate in top of double boiler over hot, not boiling, water. Remove from heat; cool. Beat butter, granulated sugar, egg, vanilla and salt in large bowl until light and fluffy. Blend in melted chocolate. Add flour; beat until stiff. Fit cookie press with your choice of plate. Load press with dough; press cookies 2 inches apart onto prepared cookie sheets.

2. Bake 5 to 7 minutes or until very lightly browned around edges. Remove to wire racks to cool. Sprinkle with cocoa powder.

Makes about 5 dozen cookies

*Clockwise from top left: Chocolate Spritz,
Fruit and Nut Chippers (page 42),
Lemon Melts (page 61) and
Classic Chocolate Chunk Cookies (page 52)*

Patchwork Cream Cheese Cookies

½ cup (1 stick) butter or margarine, softened
3 ounces cream cheese, softened
½ cup granulated sugar
1 large egg
1 teaspoon grated orange zest
1 teaspoon vanilla extract
2 cups all-purpose flour
½ teaspoon baking soda
1¾ cups "M&M's"® Chocolate Mini Baking Bits
    Granulated sugar

Preheat oven to 350°F. Cream butter, cream cheese and sugar until light and fluffy; add egg, orange zest and vanilla. Combine flour and baking soda; blend into creamed mixture. Stir in "M&M's"® Chocolate Mini Baking Bits. Shape dough into 1-inch balls; place about 2 inches apart onto greased cookie sheets. Gently flatten cookies with bottom of greased glass dipped in sugar. Bake 12 to 15 minutes.   *Makes about 3 dozen cookies*

Eggnog Crisps

½ cup (1 stick) butter or margarine, softened
1 cup granulated sugar
1 large egg
1½ teaspoons brandy extract
1½ cups cake flour
½ cup ground pecans
½ teaspoon ground nutmeg
1¾ cups "M&M's"® Chocolate Mini Baking Bits
36 pecan halves

Preheat oven to 375°F. Cream butter and sugar until light and fluffy; add egg and brandy extract. Combine flour, ground pecans and nutmeg; blend into creamed mixture. Stir in "M&M's"® Chocolate Mini Baking Bits. Drop by heaping tablespoonfuls onto greased cookie sheets; top each with 1 pecan half. Bake 10 to 11 minutes or until edges turn light golden. Cool 1 minute on cookie sheets.   *Makes about 3 dozen cookies*

Left to right: Patchwork Cream Cheese Cookies and Eggnog Crisps

Mexican Chocolate Macaroons

8 squares (1 ounce each) semisweet chocolate, divided
1¾ cups plus ⅓ cup whole almonds, divided
¾ cup sugar
2 egg whites
1 teaspoon ground cinnamon
1 teaspoon vanilla

1. Preheat oven to 400°F. Grease cookie sheets.

2. Place 5 squares chocolate in food processor; process until coarsely chopped. Add 1¾ cups almonds and sugar; process using on/off pulsing action until mixture is finely ground. Add egg whites, cinnamon and vanilla; process just until mixture forms moist dough.

3. Shape dough into 1-inch balls. (Dough will be sticky.) Place 2 inches apart on prepared cookie sheets. Press 1 whole almond into center of each dough ball.

4. Bake 8 to 10 minutes or just until set. Cool 2 minutes on cookie sheets. Remove to wire racks; cool completely.

5. Place remaining 3 squares chocolate in small resealable food storage bag; seal. Microwave on HIGH 1 minute; knead bag. Microwave at additional 30-second intervals until chocolate is melted, kneading after each interval. Cut off small corner of bag; drizzle chocolate over cookies. Let stand until set. Store in airtight containers.

Makes about 3 dozen cookies

Mexican Chocolate Macaroons

Hot Chocolate Cookies

½ cup (1 stick) butter, softened
½ cup sugar
¼ teaspoon salt
1 cup milk chocolate chips, melted, divided
1 cup all-purpose flour
   Mini marshmallows, cut into small pieces

1. Preheat oven to 350°F. Lightly grease cookie sheets or line with parchment paper.

2. Beat butter, sugar and salt in large bowl until well blended. Add ¼ cup melted chocolate; beat until well blended. Gradually add flour, beating after each addition.

3. Shape dough by level tablespoonfuls into balls. (If dough is too soft, refrigerate 1 hour or until firm enough to handle.) Place 2 inches apart on prepared cookie sheets; flatten to ½-inch thickness. Bake 15 to 17 minutes or until firm. Cool on cookie sheets 5 minutes. Remove to wire racks; cool completely.

4. Spread about 1 teaspoon remaining melted chocolate onto each cookie. Sprinkle with marshmallow pieces; press gently into chocolate. Refrigerate at least 1 hour or until set.   *Makes about 2 dozen cookies*

Hot Chocolate Cookies

Fruit and Nut Chippers

1 cup (2 sticks) butter, softened
¾ cup granulated sugar
¾ cup packed light brown sugar
2 eggs
1 teaspoon vanilla
2¼ cups all-purpose flour
1 teaspoon baking soda
½ teaspoon salt
1 package (about 12 ounces) milk chocolate chips
1 cup chopped dried apricots
1 cup chopped pecans or walnuts

1. Preheat oven to 375°F.

2. Beat butter, granulated sugar and brown sugar in large bowl until light and fluffy. Beat in eggs and vanilla. Combine flour, baking soda and salt in medium bowl; add to butter mixture. Beat until well blended. Stir in chocolate chips, apricots and pecans.

3. Drop dough by heaping teaspoonfuls 2 inches apart onto ungreased cookie sheets. Bake 9 to 10 minutes or until edges are golden brown. Let cookies stand on cookie sheets 2 minutes. Remove cookies to wire racks; cool completely.   *Makes about 5 dozen cookies*

Helpful Hint

Store soft and crisp cookies separately at room temperature to prevent changes in texture and flavor. Keep soft cookies in airtight containers. Store crisp cookies in containers with loose-fitting lids to prevent moisture buildup.

Pumpkin Oatmeal Cookies

1 cup all-purpose flour
1 teaspoon ground cinnamon
½ teaspoon salt
½ teaspoon ground nutmeg
¼ teaspoon baking soda
1½ cups packed light brown sugar
½ cup (1 stick) butter, softened
1 egg
1 teaspoon vanilla
½ cup solid-pack pumpkin
2 cups uncooked old-fashioned oats
1 cup dried cranberries (optional)

1. Preheat oven to 350°F. Line cookie sheets with parchment paper.

2. Sift flour, cinnamon, salt, nutmeg and baking soda into medium bowl. Beat brown sugar and butter in large bowl with electric mixer at medium speed about 5 minutes or until light and fluffy. Beat in egg and vanilla. Add pumpkin; beat at low speed until blended. Beat in flour mixture just until blended. Add oats; mix well. Stir in cranberries, if desired.

3. Drop batter by generous tablespoonfuls about 2 inches apart onto prepared cookie sheets.

4. Bake 12 minutes or until golden brown. Cool on cookie sheets 1 minute; remove to wire racks to cool completely.   *Makes about 2 dozen cookies*

Snowball Surprises

1 cup (2 sticks) butter, softened
¾ cup powdered sugar, divided
1 teaspoon vanilla
1¾ cups all-purpose flour
¼ teaspoon salt
1 cup pecan halves, toasted* and finely chopped
1 bar (3 ounces) chocolate candy with almonds, broken into
    36 (½-inch) pieces

To toast pecans, spread in single layer on cookie sheet. Bake in preheated 350°F oven 8 to 10 minutes or until golden brown, stirring frequently.

1. Lightly grease cookie sheets or line with parchment paper. Beat butter and ½ cup powdered sugar in large bowl until well blended. Add vanilla; beat until blended. Gradually add flour and salt, beating after each addition. Stir in pecans.

2. Shape dough by tablespoonfuls into 36 balls. Press chocolate piece into each dough ball, working dough around chocolate to cover. Place balls 1½ inches apart on prepared cookie sheets. Refrigerate 30 minutes to 1 hour or until dough is firm.

3. Preheat oven to 350°F. Bake cookies 13 to 15 minutes or until edges are lightly browned. Remove to wire racks; cool slightly. Sprinkle remaining ¼ cup powdered sugar over warm cookies.   *Makes 3 dozen cookies*

Snowball Surprises

Cashew-Lemon Shortbread Cookies

½ **cup roasted cashews**
1 **cup (2 sticks) butter, softened**
½ **cup sugar**
2 **teaspoons lemon extract**
1 **teaspoon vanilla**
2 **cups all-purpose flour**
   Additional sugar

Preheat oven to 325°F. Place cashews in bowl of food processor; process until finely ground. Add butter, sugar, extract and vanilla; process until well blended. Add flour; process using on/off pulses until dough is well blended and begins to form a ball. Shape dough into 1½-inch balls; roll in additional sugar. Place balls about 2 inches apart on ungreased cookie sheets; flatten slightly with bottom of glass dipped in sugar. Bake 17 to 19 minutes or just until set and edges are lightly browned. Remove to wire racks to cool.

Makes 2 to 2½ dozen cookies

Chunky Butter Christmas Cookies

1¼ **cups butter, softened**
1 **cup packed brown sugar**
½ **cup dairy sour cream**
1 **egg**
2 **teaspoons vanilla**
1½ **cups all-purpose flour**
1 **teaspoon** *each* **baking soda and salt**
1½ **cups old-fashioned or quick oats, uncooked**
1 **(10-ounce) package white chocolate pieces**
1 **cup flaked coconut**
1 **(3½-ounce) jar macadamia nuts, coarsely chopped**

Beat butter and sugar in large bowl until light and fluffy. Blend in sour cream, egg and vanilla. Add combined flour, baking soda and salt; mix well. Stir in oats, white chocolate pieces, coconut and nuts. Drop rounded teaspoonfuls of dough, 2 inches apart, onto ungreased cookie sheets. Bake in preheated 375°F oven 10 to 12 minutes or until edges are lightly browned. Cool 1 minute; remove to cooling racks.

Makes 5 dozen cookies

Favorite recipe from **Wisconsin Milk Marketing Board**

Cashew-Lemon Shortbread Cookies

Ginger Spice Thumbprints

½ cup (1 stick) butter, softened
¾ cup packed light brown sugar
¼ cup molasses
1 egg
2¼ cups all-purpose flour
1¾ teaspoons ground ginger
1½ teaspoons ground cinnamon
1 teaspoon baking soda
¼ teaspoon salt
   Granulated sugar
½ cup fig, plum or any flavor preserves

1. Preheat oven to 350°F. Lightly grease cookie sheets or line with parchment paper.

2. Beat butter and brown sugar in large bowl with electric mixer at medium speed until well blended. Add molasses and egg; beat until well blended. Combine flour, ginger, cinnamon, baking soda and salt in medium bowl; gradually add to butter mixture, beating after each addition.

3. Place granulated sugar in shallow bowl. Shape dough into 1-inch balls; roll in sugar to coat. Place balls 1½ inches apart on prepared cookie sheets. Press center of each ball with thumb; fill each thumbprint with ½ teaspoon preserves.

4. Bake cookies about 13 minutes or until edges are lightly browned. Cool on cookie sheets 1 minute. Remove to wire racks; cool completely.

Makes about 4 dozen cookies

Ginger Spice Thumbprints

Holiday Double Peanut Butter Fudge Cookies

1 can (14 ounces) sweetened condensed milk (not evaporated milk)
¾ cup REESE'S® Creamy Peanut Butter
2 cups all-purpose biscuit baking mix
1 teaspoon vanilla extract
¾ cup REESE'S® Peanut Butter Chips
¼ cup granulated sugar
½ teaspoon red colored sugar
½ teaspoon green colored sugar

1. Heat oven to 375°F.

2. Beat sweetened condensed milk and peanut butter with electric mixer on medium speed in large bowl until smooth. Beat in baking mix and vanilla; stir in peanut butter chips. Set aside.

3. Stir together granulated sugar and colored sugars in small bowl. Shape dough into 1-inch balls; roll in sugar. Place 2 inches apart on ungreased cookie sheet; flatten slightly with bottom of glass.

4. Bake 6 to 8 minutes or until very lightly browned (do not overbake). Cool slightly. Remove to wire rack and cool completely. Store in tightly covered container.   *Makes about 3½ dozen cookies*

Holiday Double Peanut Butter Fudge Cookies

Classic Chocolate Chunk Cookies

1⅔ cups all-purpose flour
¾ teaspoon baking soda
½ teaspoon salt
¾ cup (1½ sticks) butter, softened
½ cup granulated sugar
½ cup packed brown sugar
½ teaspoon vanilla
1 egg
1 package (12 ounces) semisweet chocolate chunks or chips
1 cup chopped nuts

1. Preheat oven to 375°F.

2. Combine flour, baking soda and salt in small bowl. Beat butter, granulated sugar, brown sugar and vanilla in large bowl with electric mixer at medium speed until light and creamy. Add egg; mix well. Gradually add flour mixture, beating until well blended. Stir in chocolate chunks and nuts. Drop by tablespoonfuls 2 inches apart onto ungreased cookie sheets.

3. Bake about 11 minutes or until light golden brown. Cool 1 minute on cookie sheets; remove to wire racks to cool completely.

Makes about 3 dozen cookies

Classic Chocolate Chunk Pan Cookies: Prepare dough as directed; spread dough in greased 13×9-inch baking pan. Bake at 375°F for 20 to 22 minutes or until golden brown. Cool completely in pan on wire rack.

Helpful Hint

To have freshly baked cookies at a moment's notice, prepare the dough as directed. Freeze heaping tablespoonfuls of dough on a cookie sheet for about 1 hour, then freeze them in a resealable freezer food storage bag for up to 1 month. Bake the frozen cookie dough on ungreased cookie sheets at 375°F for 15 to 16 minutes or until golden brown.

Ho Ho Surprises

48 red or green maraschino cherries (about one 16-ounce jar)
  1 cup butter or margarine, softened
  ⅓ cup confectioners' sugar
  ½ teaspoon almond extract
2¼ cups all-purpose flour
  ¼ teaspoon salt
  ½ cup finely chopped pecans
    Confectioners' sugar

Drain maraschino cherries thoroughly on paper towels; set aside. Combine butter and ⅓ cup confectioners' sugar in a large mixing bowl. Beat with an electric mixer on medium speed 3 to 4 minutes or until well mixed. Stir in almond extract. Add flour and salt; mix well. Stir in pecans.

Shape about 2 teaspoons dough around each cherry. Place on an ungreased cookie sheet about 1 inch apart. Bake in a preheated 375°F oven 12 to 15 minutes or until set but not brown. Roll in confectioners' sugar while still warm. Let cool. If desired, roll in confectioners' sugar again.

Makes 4 dozen cookies

Favorite recipe from **Cherry Marketing Institute**

Flourless Peanut Butter Cookies

1 cup packed light brown sugar
1 cup peanut butter
1 egg
24 milk chocolate candy stars or milk chocolate candy kisses

1. Preheat oven to 350°F. Beat brown sugar, peanut butter and egg in medium bowl until blended and smooth.

2. Shape dough into 24 (1½ inch) balls; place 2 inches apart on ungreased cookie sheets. Press 1 chocolate star into each ball. Bake 10 to 12 minutes or until set. Transfer to wire racks; cool completely.

Makes about 2 dozen cookies

Chunky Nut Blondie Drops

1¼ cups packed light brown sugar
1 cup (2 sticks) butter, softened
½ cup granulated sugar
2 eggs
1½ teaspoons vanilla
2½ cups all-purpose flour
1 teaspoon baking powder
½ teaspoon salt
¼ teaspoon baking soda
1½ cups coarsely chopped chocolate squares or nuggets with truffle
    or caramel centers
1¼ cups coarsely chopped pecans, toasted*
1¼ cups coarsely chopped walnuts, toasted*

*To toast nuts, spread in single layer on cookie sheet. Bake in preheated 350°F oven 8 to 10 minutes or until golden brown, stirring frequently.

1. Preheat oven to 350°F. Line cookie sheets with parchment paper.

2. Beat brown sugar, butter and granulated sugar in large bowl with electric mixer at medium speed until well blended. Add eggs and vanilla; beat until well blended. Combine flour, baking powder, salt and baking soda in small bowl; gradually add to butter mixture, beating after each addition. Stir in candy and nuts.

3. Drop dough by rounded tablespoonfuls about 1½ inches apart onto prepared cookie sheets. (If dough is too soft, refrigerate about 1 hour before baking.)

4. Bake 15 to 17 minutes or until golden brown. Cool on cookie sheets 2 minutes. Remove to wire racks; cool completely.

Makes about 4 dozen cookies

Chunky Nut Blondie Drops

Melt-in-Your-Mouth Christmas Marbles

½ cup (1 stick) butter, softened
6 tablespoons powdered sugar
¼ teaspoon vanilla
1 cup minus 2 tablespoons all-purpose flour
¼ teaspoon salt
Red and green food coloring

1. Preheat oven to 350°F. Lightly grease cookie sheets or line with parchment paper.

2. Beat butter and powdered sugar in large bowl with electric mixer at medium speed until light and fluffy. Beat in vanilla until well blended. Gradually add flour and salt, beating after each addition.

3. Transfer half of dough to medium bowl; add red food coloring, beating until well blended and desired shade is reached. Add green food coloring to remaining dough half, beating until well blended and desired shade is reached.

4. For each marble, shape ½ teaspoonful of each color dough into one ball; place 1 inch apart on prepared cookie sheets. Bake 12 to 14 minutes or until edges are lightly browned. Cool on cookie sheets 2 minutes. Remove to wire racks; cool completely.   *Makes about 4 dozen cookies*

Tip: To get the brightest colors, tint the dough with paste food coloring. Add a small amount of the paste with a toothpick, then stir well. Gradually add more color until the dough reaches the desired shade. Paste food coloring is sold at specialty stores and come in a wide variety of colors.

Chocolate Raspberry Thumbprints

1½ cups (3 sticks) butter, softened
1 cup granulated sugar
1 egg
1 teaspoon vanilla
3 cups all-purpose flour
¼ cup unsweetened cocoa powder
½ teaspoon salt
1 cup (6 ounces) mini semisweet chocolate chips (optional)
⅔ cup raspberry preserves
Powdered sugar (optional)

1. Preheat oven to 350°F. Grease cookie sheets.

2. Beat butter and sugar in large bowl. Beat in egg and vanilla until light and fluffy. Mix in flour, cocoa and salt until well blended. Stir in mini chocolate chips, if desired.

3. Shape level tablespoonfuls of dough into balls. Place 2 inches apart on prepared cookie sheets. Make deep indentation in center of each ball with thumb.

4. Bake 12 to 15 minutes until just set. Cool 2 minutes on cookie sheets. Remove to wire racks; cool completely.

5. Fill centers with raspberry preserves and sprinkle with powdered sugar.

Makes about 4½ dozen cookies

 ## Helpful Hint

To soften butter or margarine more quickly, cut the sticks into small pieces and let them stand at room temperature. Or, place 1 stick of butter on a microwavable plate and heat on LOW (30%) about 30 seconds or just until softened.

Chocolate Raspberry Thumbprints

Nutmeg Molasses Cookies

1½ **cups sugar**
 1 **cup shortening**
 ⅓ **cup molasses**
 1 **teaspoon vanilla**
 2 **eggs**
 3 **cups all-purpose flour**
 2 **teaspoons baking soda**
 1 **teaspoon ground nutmeg**
 1 **teaspoon ground cinnamon**
 ½ **teaspoon salt**
   Additional sugar

1. Preheat oven to 350°F.

2. Beat sugar, shortening, molasses and vanilla in large bowl with electric mixer at medium speed until creamy. Add eggs, one at a time, beating well after each addition.

3. Combine flour, baking soda, nutmeg, cinnamon and salt in medium bowl; gradually add to shortening mixture, beating at low speed until blended. Beat at medium speed until thick dough forms.

4. Shape dough into 1½-inch balls. Place 3 inches apart on ungreased cookie sheets. Flatten with bottom of glass dipped in sugar.

5. Bake 10 minutes or until cookies look dry. Cool completely on wire racks.   *Makes about 5 dozen cookies*

Lemon Melts

½ **cup canola oil**
½ **cup (1 stick) butter, melted**
½ **cup powdered sugar**
½ **cup packed brown sugar**
1 **tablespoon fresh lemon juice**
1 **tablespoon vanilla**
1½ **teaspoons almond extract**
2 **cups all-purpose flour**
½ **teaspoon cream of tartar**
½ **teaspoon baking soda**

1. Preheat oven to 350°F. Grease cookie sheets.

2. Beat oil, butter, sugars, lemon juice, vanilla and almond extract in large bowl with electric mixer at medium speed until smooth.

3. Combine flour, cream of tartar and baking soda in small bowl. Gradually beat into butter mixture until stiff dough forms.

4. Drop dough by rounded tablespoonfuls 2 inches apart onto prepared cookie sheets; flatten gently with fork. Bake 20 minutes or until edges are lightly browned. Cool on cookie sheets 1 minute. Remove to wire racks; cool completely. *Makes about 3½ dozen cookies*

 Helpful Hint

One medium lemon will yield
about 3 to 4 tablespoons of juice.
If only a small amount of juice is needed, make a
hole in the lemon with a toothpick. Squeeze out the
amount you need, then seal the hole by re-inserting
the toothpick; store in the refrigerator.

Cappuccino Spice Cookies

2½ teaspoons instant coffee granules
1 tablespoon boiling water
1 cup (2 sticks) butter, softened
1 cup packed light brown sugar
½ cup granulated sugar
2 eggs
1 teaspoon vanilla
2⅔ cups all-purpose flour
1 teaspoon baking soda
¾ teaspoon ground cinnamon
½ teaspoon salt
¼ teaspoon ground nutmeg or ground cloves
3 cups double chocolate or semisweet chocolate chips

1. Preheat oven to 375°F.

2. Dissolve coffee granules in boiling water. Beat butter and sugars in large bowl with electric mixer at medium speed until fluffy. Add eggs, coffee and vanilla; beat until well blended.

3. Combine flour, baking soda, cinnamon, salt and nutmeg in medium bowl; gradually add to butter mixture, beating at low speed until well blended. Stir in chocolate chips.

4. Drop dough by heaping tablespoonfuls 2 inches apart onto ungreased cookie sheets. Bake 8 to 10 minutes or until set. Let stand on cookie sheets 1 minute; transfer to wire racks to cool completely.

Makes about 3½ dozen cookies

Cappuccino Spice Minis: Prepare dough as directed above; drop by heaping teaspoonfuls onto ungreased cookie sheets. Bake 7 minutes or until set. Makes about 7 dozen mini cookies.

Cappuccino Spice Cookies

Sugarplum Fun

Crunchy Christmas Wreaths

22 red licorice strings (about 10 inches long)
½ cup (1 stick) butter
3 cups mini marshmallows
1 teaspoon vanilla
¼ teaspoon salt
Green food coloring
5 to 5½ cups puffed corn cereal
⅓ cup mini candy-coated chocolate pieces (optional)

1. Line cookie sheets with waxed paper. Tie each licorice string into bow; set aside.

2. Melt butter in large heavy saucepan over low heat. Add marshmallows; stir until melted and smooth. Stir in vanilla and salt. Tint with food coloring until desired shade is reached. Add 5 cups cereal; stir until evenly coated. Add remaining ½ cup cereal if necessary. Remove from heat.

3. Drop mixture by ¼ cupfuls onto prepared cookie sheets. With lightly greased hands, quickly shape each mound into 3-inch ring. Press licorice and candies onto each wreath as desired. Refrigerate 1 hour or until set. Store covered in refrigerator. *Makes 22 wreaths*

Clockwise from top left: Crunchy Christmas Wreaths, Chocolate Gingerbread Cookies (page 69), Angels (page 68) and Buche De Noel Cookies (page 78)

Ornament Brownies

6 squares (1 ounce each) semisweet chocolate, coarsely chopped
1 tablespoon instant coffee granules
1 tablespoon boiling water
¾ cup all-purpose flour
¾ teaspoon ground cinnamon
½ teaspoon baking powder
¼ teaspoon salt
½ cup sugar
¼ cup (½ stick) butter, softened
2 eggs
  Prepared white frosting
  Assorted food coloring
  Small candy canes
  Assorted candies and sprinkles

1. Preheat oven to 350°F. Grease 8-inch square baking pan. Place chocolate in small microwavable bowl. Microwave on HIGH 30 seconds; stir. Repeat as necessary until chocolate is melted; set aside. Dissolve coffee granules in boiling water; set aside.

2. Combine flour, cinnamon, baking powder and salt in small bowl. Beat sugar and butter in large bowl with electric mixer at medium speed until light and fluffy. Beat in eggs, one at a time. Beat in melted chocolate and coffee until well blended. Add flour mixture, beating at low speed until well blended. Spread batter evenly in prepared pan.

3. Bake 30 to 35 minutes or until center is set. Remove to wire rack; cool completely. Cut into holiday shapes using 2-inch cookie cutters.

4. Tint frosting with food coloring to desired colors. Spread over each brownie. Break off top of small candy cane to create loop; insert in top of brownie. Decorate as desired with assorted candies and sprinkles.

Makes about 8 brownies

Ornament Brownies

Angels

Butter Cookie Dough (recipe follows)
1 egg, lightly beaten
Small pretzels, white icing, toasted coconut, edible glitter and
assorted small decors

1. Prepare and chill Butter Cookie Dough as directed.

2. Preheat oven to 350°F. Grease cookie sheets. Roll dough on floured surface to ¼-inch thickness. Cut out 12 (4-inch) triangles. Reroll scraps to ¼-inch thickness. Cut out 12 (1½-inch) circles.

3. Place triangles on prepared cookie sheets. Brush with beaten egg. Attach circle, pressing gently. Bake 8 to 10 minutes or just until edges begin to brown. Remove to wire racks; cool completely.

4. Attach pretzels to back of each cookie for wings using icing as "glue." Let stand 30 minutes or until icing is set. Pipe icing around hairline of each angel; sprinkle with coconut and glitter.

5. Decorate cookies with icing, coconut, glitter and decors to resemble angels as desired. Let cookies stand 1 hour or until icing is set.

Makes 1 dozen cookies

Butter Cookie Dough

¾ cup (1½ sticks) butter, softened
¼ cup granulated sugar
¼ cup packed light brown sugar
1 egg yolk
1¾ cups all-purpose flour
¾ teaspoon baking powder
⅛ teaspoon salt

1. Beat butter, granulated sugar, brown sugar and egg yolk in medium bowl until well blended. Add flour, baking powder and salt; beat until well blended.

2. Cover; refrigerate about 4 hours or until firm.

Chocolate Gingerbread Cookies

½ cup (1 stick) butter, softened
½ cup packed light brown sugar
¼ cup granulated sugar
1 tablespoon shortening
4 squares (1 ounce each) semisweet chocolate, melted and cooled
2 tablespoons molasses
1 egg
2¼ cups all-purpose flour
3 tablespoons unsweetened cocoa powder
2½ teaspoons ground ginger
½ teaspoon baking soda
½ teaspoon ground cinnamon
⅛ teaspoon salt
⅛ teaspoon finely ground black pepper
Prepared icing (optional)

1. Beat butter, sugars and shortening in large bowl with electric mixer at medium speed until creamy. Add chocolate; beat until blended. Add molasses and egg; beat until well blended.

2. Combine flour, cocoa, ginger, baking soda, cinnamon, salt and pepper in medium bowl; gradually add to butter mixture, beating until well blended. Divide dough in half. Wrap each half in plastic wrap; refrigerate at least 1 hour.

3. Preheat oven to 350°F. Roll out half of dough between sheets of plastic wrap to ¼-inch thickness. Cut dough with 5-inch cookie cutters; place on ungreased cookie sheets. Refrigerate at least 15 minutes. Repeat with remaining dough.

4. Bake 8 to 10 minutes or until cookies have puffed slightly and have small cracks on tops. Cool 5 minutes on cookie sheets; remove to wire racks to cool completely. Decorate with icing as desired.

Makes about 2 dozen 5-inch cookies

Chewy Chocolate Gingerbread Drops: Decrease flour to 1¾ cups. Shape 1½ teaspoonfuls of dough into balls. Place on ungreased cookie sheets. Flatten balls slightly. Do not refrigerate before baking. Bake as directed above. Makes about 4½ dozen cookies.

Pink Poinsettias

1 cup (2 sticks) butter, softened
⅔ cup sugar
1 teaspoon vanilla
½ teaspoon peppermint extract
1¾ cups all-purpose flour
½ teaspoon baking powder
¼ teaspoon salt
    Red or pink food coloring
    Yellow decorating sugar

1. Lightly grease cookie sheets or line with parchment paper.

2. Beat butter and sugar in large bowl with electric mixer at medium speed until well blended. Add vanilla and peppermint extract; beat until well blended. Combine flour, baking powder and salt in medium bowl; gradually add to butter mixture, beating after each addition. Reserve ½ cup dough. Tint remaining dough with food coloring until desired shade is reached.

3. For flower centers, shape reserved plain dough into 30 small balls; roll in yellow sugar. Place 2 inches apart on prepared cookie sheets. Flatten to ⅓-inch thickness.

4. For flower petals, divide pink dough into 30 pieces. Shape each piece into 8 ovals; place in circle around flower center on cookie sheet. Pinch outside ends of ovals into points for petal shapes. Refrigerate at least 15 minutes or until firm.

5. Preheat oven to 275°F. Bake about 30 minutes or until cookies are set and edges are lightly browned. Cool on cookie sheets 2 minutes. Remove to wire racks; cool completely.   *Makes 2½ dozen cookies*

Pink Poinsettias

Ice Skates

½ cup (1 stick) butter, softened
1¼ cups honey
1 cup packed light brown sugar
1 egg, separated
5½ cups self-rising flour
1 teaspoon ground ginger
1 teaspoon ground cinnamon
½ cup milk
Prepared colored icing, sprinkles and small candy canes

1. Beat butter, honey, brown sugar and egg yolk in large bowl with electric mixer at medium speed until light and fluffy.

2. Combine flour, ginger and cinnamon in small bowl. Add alternately with milk to butter mixture; beat just until blended. Wrap in plastic wrap; refrigerate 30 minutes.

3. Preheat oven to 350°F. Grease cookie sheets.

4. Roll dough on lightly floured surface to ¼-inch thickness. Cut dough using 3½-inch boot-shaped cookie cutter. Place cutouts 2 inches apart on prepared cookie sheets.

5. Bake 8 to 10 minutes or until edges are lightly browned. Cool on cookie sheets 2 minutes. Remove to wire racks; cool completely.

6. Decorate cookies with colored icing and sprinkles, attaching candy canes as skate blades with additional icing.   *Makes about 4 dozen cookies*

Helpful Hint

If you don't have a boot-shaped cookie cutter, make a pattern using clean, lightweight cardboard. Using the photo as a guide, draw the pattern on the cardboard. Cut out the pattern and lightly spray one side with nonstick cooking spray. Place the pattern, sprayed side down, on the rolled-out dough; cut around it with a sharp knife.

Ice Skates

Snowmen

1 package (18 ounces) refrigerated chocolate chip cookie dough
1½ cups sifted powdered sugar
2 tablespoons milk
Assorted candies and decors

1. Preheat oven to 375°F. Cut dough into 12 equal sections. Shape each section into 3 balls: small, medium and large. For each snowman, place 1 small, 1 medium and 1 large ball ¼ inch apart on ungreased cookie sheet.

2. Bake 10 to 12 minutes or until edges are very lightly browned. Cool 4 minutes on cookie sheets. Remove to wire racks to cool completely.

3. Mix powdered sugar and milk in medium bowl until smooth. Pour glaze evenly over cookies. Let cookies stand 20 minutes or until set. Decorate as desired. *Makes 1 dozen cookies*

Festive Candy Canes

¾ cup (1½ sticks) butter, softened
1 cup powdered sugar
1 egg
1 teaspoon peppermint extract
½ teaspoon vanilla
1⅔ cups all-purpose flour
⅛ teaspoon salt
Red food coloring

1. Preheat oven to 350°F. Beat butter and powdered sugar in large bowl until light and fluffy. Add egg, peppermint extract and vanilla; beat until well blended. Add flour and salt; beat until well blended. (Dough will be sticky.)

2. Divide dough in half. Tint half of dough with food coloring to desired shade. Leave remaining dough plain.

3. For each candy cane, with floured hands, shape heaping teaspoonful of each color dough into 5-inch rope. Twist together into candy cane shape. Place 2 inches apart on ungreased cookie sheets.

4. Bake 7 to 8 minutes or until set and edges are lightly browned. Cool on cookie sheets 2 minutes. Remove to wire racks to cool completely.
Makes about 2 dozen cookies

Snowmen

Christmas Tree Treats

¾ cup plus 2 tablespoons (1¼ sticks) butter, softened
½ cup sugar
½ teaspoon almond extract
1¾ cups all-purpose flour
½ teaspoon baking powder
¼ teaspoon salt
   Green food coloring
18 flat wooden popsicle sticks (at least 5 inches long)
   Assorted decorating icing and decors (optional)

1. Beat butter and sugar in large bowl with electric mixer at medium speed until well blended. Add almond extract; beat until well blended. Combine flour, baking powder and salt; gradually add to butter mixture, beating after each addition. Tint with food coloring until desired shade is reached. Divide dough in half; shape each half into 1-inch-wide oval log. Wrap in plastic wrap; refrigerate 2 hours or until firm.

2. Preheat oven to 275°F. Lightly grease cookie sheets or line with parchment paper. Place wooden sticks on prepared cookie sheets. Cut dough into ¼-inch-thick slices. For each tree, place 3 slices next to each other half way up from bottom of stick; place 2 slices above them, overlapping bottom slices slightly. Place 1 slice at top of tree, overlapping middle slices slightly.

3. Bake about 30 minutes or until edges are lightly browned. Cool on cookie sheets 5 minutes. Remove to wire racks; cool completely. Decorate with icing and decors as desired.   *Makes 1½ dozen large cookies*

Helpful Hint

Extracts are very concentrated flavorings derived from a variety of foods. A wide assortment of extracts and flavorings are available in the spice section of the supermarket. To change the taste of these cookies, use another extract, such as lemon, instead of the almond extract.

Buche De Noel Cookies

⅔ cup butter or margarine, softened
1 cup granulated sugar
2 eggs
2 teaspoons vanilla extract
2½ cups all-purpose flour
½ cup HERSHEY'S Cocoa
½ teaspoon baking soda
¼ teaspoon salt
   Mocha Frosting (recipe follows)
   Powdered sugar (optional)

1. Beat butter and sugar with electric mixer on medium speed in large bowl until well blended. Add eggs and vanilla; beat until fluffy. Stir together flour, cocoa, baking soda and salt; gradually add to butter mixture, beating until well blended. Cover; refrigerate dough 1 to 2 hours.

2. Heat oven to 350°F. Shape heaping teaspoons of dough into logs about 2½ inches long and ¾ inches in diameter; place on ungreased cookie sheet. Bake 7 to 9 minutes or until set. Cool slightly. Remove to wire rack and cool completely.

3. Frost cookies with Mocha Frosting. Using tines of fork, draw lines through frosting to imitate tree bark. Lightly dust with powdered sugar, if desired. *Makes about 2½ dozen cookies*

Mocha Frosting

6 tablespoons butter or margarine, softened
2⅔ cups powdered sugar
⅓ cup HERSHEY'S Cocoa
3 to 4 tablespoons milk
2 teaspoons powdered instant espresso dissolved in 1 teaspoon
   hot water
1 teaspoon vanilla extract

Beat butter with electric mixer on medium speed in medium bowl until creamy. Add powdered sugar and cocoa alternately with milk, dissolved espresso and vanilla, beating to spreadable consistency.

Makes about 1⅔ cups frosting

Danish Cookie Rings

½ cup blanched almonds
2 cups all-purpose flour
¾ cup sugar
¼ teaspoon baking powder
1 cup (2 sticks) butter, cut into small pieces
1 egg
1 tablespoon milk
1 tablespoon vanilla
15 candied red cherries
15 candied green cherries

1. Grease cookie sheets; set aside. Process almonds in food processor until ground but not pasty. Place almonds, flour, sugar and baking powder in large bowl. Cut butter into flour mixture with pastry blender or 2 knives until mixture is crumbly.

2. Beat egg, milk and vanilla in small bowl with fork until well blended. Add egg mixture to flour mixture; stir until soft dough forms.

3. Spoon dough into pastry bag fitted with medium star tip. Pipe 3-inch rings 2 inches apart on prepared cookie sheets. Refrigerate rings 15 minutes or until firm.

4. Preheat oven to 375°F. Cut red cherries into quarters. Cut green cherries into halves; cut each half into 4 slivers. Press red cherry quarter onto each ring where ends meet. Arrange 2 green cherry slivers on either side of red cherry to form leaves. Bake 8 to 10 minutes or until golden. Remove to wire racks to cool completely.   *Makes about 5 dozen cookies*

Little Christmas Puddings

1 can (14 ounces) sweetened condensed milk
1 square (1 ounce) semisweet chocolate
2 teaspoons vanilla
2¼ cups chocolate sandwich cookie crumbs
⅓ cup white chocolate chips
Red and green holly decors

1. Combine sweetened condensed milk and semisweet chocolate in medium saucepan; cook and stir over low heat until chocolate is melted and mixture is smooth. Remove from heat; stir in vanilla.

2. Stir cookie crumbs into chocolate mixture until well blended. Cover with plastic wrap; refrigerate 1 hour.

3. Line baking sheet with waxed paper. Shape heaping teaspoonfuls crumb mixture into 1-inch balls. Place on prepared baking sheet. Refrigerate until firm.

4. Place balls in 1¾-inch foil or paper baking cups. Place white chocolate chips in microwavable bowl. Microwave on MEDIUM (50%) about 2 minutes or until melted, stirring after each minute. Spoon melted white chocolate over tops of balls. Decorate with decors. Let stand until set.

Makes about 3½ dozen puddings

Little Christmas Puddings

Candy-Studded Wreaths

1 cup (2 sticks) butter, softened
½ cup powdered sugar
2 tablespoons packed light brown sugar
1 teaspoon vanilla
¼ teaspoon salt
2 cups all-purpose flour
Green food coloring
Mini candy-coated chocolate pieces

1. Beat butter, powdered sugar, brown sugar, vanilla and salt in large bowl with electric mixer at medium speed 2 minutes or until light and fluffy. Add flour, ½ cup at a time, beating well after each addition.

2. Divide dough in half. Tint half of dough with food coloring to desired shade. Leave remaining dough plain. (If dough is too soft, wrap in plastic wrap and refrigerate about 1 hour.)

3. Preheat oven to 300°F. Shape green dough into 28 (5-inch) ropes. Repeat with plain dough. For each wreath, twist one green and one plain rope together; press ends together. Place on ungreased cookie sheet. Press 4 to 6 chocolate pieces into each wreath.

4. Bake 15 to 18 minutes or until lightly browned. Cool 5 minutes on cookie sheets; transfer to wire racks to cool completely.   *Makes 28 cookies*

Candy-Studded Wreaths

Chocolate Reindeer

1 cup (2 sticks) butter, softened
1 cup granulated sugar
1 egg
1 teaspoon vanilla
2 squares (1 ounce each) semisweet chocolate, melted
2¼ cups all-purpose flour
1 teaspoon baking powder
¼ teaspoon salt
Assorted decorating icing, colored sugar and decors

1. Beat butter and sugar in large bowl with electric mixer at high speed until fluffy. Beat in egg and vanilla. Add chocolate; beat until well blended. Add flour, baking powder and salt; beat until well blended. Divide dough in half. Wrap each half in plastic wrap; refrigerate 2 hours or until firm.

2. Preheat oven to 325°F. Grease 2 cookie sheets.

3. Roll one half of dough on well-floured surface to ¼-inch thickness. Cut dough with 4-inch reindeer-shaped cookie cutter. Place cutouts 2 inches apart on prepared cookie sheets. Refrigerate 10 minutes.

4. Bake 13 to 15 minutes or until set. Cool completely on cookie sheets. Repeat with remaining dough.

5. Pipe icing onto cookies and decorate as desired. Let stand until set.

Makes 16 large cookies

Chocolate Reindeer

Fireside Cookie

1 package (18 ounces) refrigerated cookie dough, any flavor
Prepared icing, black licorice, gumdrops, mini chocolate chips
and assorted candies

1. Preheat oven to 350°F. Line 2 large cookie sheets with parchment paper.

2. Using about one-fourth of dough, roll into 12×3-inch strip. Trim to
11×2¼ inches; set aside. Roll remaining dough into 10×8-inch rectangle.
Trim to 9×7¾ inches; place on 1 prepared cookie sheet. Place reserved
dough strip at top of rectangle to make fireplace mantel. Roll remaining
scraps and cut into stocking shapes. Place on remaining prepared cookie
sheet.

3. Bake 10 minutes or until edges are lightly browned. Cool on cookie
sheets 5 minutes. Remove stocking cookies to wire rack. Slide large cookie
and parchment paper onto wire rack; cool completely.

4. Decorate with icing and candies as shown, attaching stockings to fireplace
cookie with icing.   *Makes 1 large cookie*

Helpful Hint

*For cutout cookies, chilled cookie
dough is easier to handle than
dough at room temperature. To minimize sticking
when using cookie cutters, dip the cutters in flour or
spray them with nonstick cooking spray before
cutting the dough.*

Fireside Cookie

Icicle Ornaments

2½ cups all-purpose flour
¼ teaspoon salt
1 cup sugar
¾ cup (1½ sticks) butter, softened
2 squares (1 ounce each) white chocolate, melted and cooled slightly
1 egg
1 teaspoon vanilla
Coarse white decorating sugar, colored sugar and decors

1. Combine flour and salt in medium bowl. Beat sugar and butter in large bowl with electric mixer at medium speed until fluffy. Beat in white chocolate, egg and vanilla. Gradually add flour mixture, beating at low speed until well blended. Shape dough into disc. Wrap in plastic wrap and refrigerate 30 minutes or until firm.

2. Preheat oven to 350°F. Grease cookie sheets. Shape heaping tablespoonfuls of dough into 10-inch ropes. Fold each rope in half; twist to make icicle shape, leaving opening at fold and tapering ends. Roll in coarse sugar; sprinkle with colored sugar and decors as desired. Place 1 inch apart on prepared cookie sheets.

3. Bake 8 to 10 minutes or until firm but not browned. Cool on cookie sheets 1 minute. Remove to wire racks; cool completely.

4. To hang cookies, pull ribbon through opening in top of each icicle and tie small knot in ribbon ends, if desired.   *Makes about 2½ dozen cookies*

Icicle Ornaments

Holiday Meringue Trees

1 cup shelled pistachio nuts
4 egg whites, at room temperature
⅛ teaspoon salt
¾ cup sugar
½ teaspoon vanilla
   Green food coloring
20 cinnamon-flavored graham cracker sticks

1. Preheat oven to 250°F. Line cookie sheets with parchment paper. Place pistachios on clean dish towel; rub to remove excess skin. Finely chop pistachios; set aside.

2. Beat egg whites and salt in large bowl until foamy. Add sugar, ¼ cup at a time, beating until soft peaks form. Add vanilla; beat until stiff and glossy. Tint with food coloring until desired shade is reached. Fold in chopped pistachios.

3. Spoon mixture into pastry bag fitted with large writing or star tip. Pipe onto prepared cookie sheets in curved lines to make 3-inch tree shapes, allowing 1½ inches between trees. Insert graham cracker stick into base of each tree for trunk.

4. Bake 40 minutes or until firm to the touch, turning cookie sheets halfway through baking time. Turn oven off; let stand in oven 1½ hours. *Do not open oven door.* Remove from oven; transfer to wire racks to cool completely.

Makes about 20 cookies

Note: Meringues are best when served within 24 hours.

Holiday Meringue Trees

Lumps of Coal

2 packages (12 ounces each) semisweet chocolate chips, divided
½ cup (1 stick) butter, cut into chunks
2 eggs
1 teaspoon vanilla
¾ cup plus 2 tablespoons sugar
⅔ cup all-purpose flour
2 tablespoons unsweetened Dutch process cocoa powder
1 teaspoon baking powder
¼ teaspoon salt

1. Lightly grease cookie sheets or line with parchment paper.

2. Combine 1 package (2 cups) chocolate chips and butter in large microwavable bowl. Microwave on HIGH 30 seconds; stir. Repeat as necessary until chips are melted and mixture is smooth. Let cool slightly.

3. Beat eggs and vanilla in large bowl with electric mixer at medium speed until blended and frothy. Add sugar; beat until thick and light. Add chocolate mixture; beat until blended. Combine flour, cocoa, baking powder and salt in medium bowl; add to butter mixture. Beat until blended. Stir in remaining chocolate chips. (Dough will be soft.)

4. Drop dough by rounded tablespoonfuls 1½ inches apart onto prepared cookie sheets. Refrigerate 30 minutes.

5. Preheat oven to 325°F. Bake 16 to 20 minutes or until cookies are firm. Cool on cookie sheets 2 minutes. Remove to wire racks; cool completely.

Makes about 2½ dozen cookies

Lumps of Coal

Jolly Bars & Brownies

Cinnamony Apple Streusel Bars

1¼ **cups all-purpose flour**
1¼ **cups graham cracker crumbs**
 ¾ **cup packed brown sugar, divided**
 ¾ **cup (1½ sticks) butter, melted**
 ¼ **cup granulated sugar**
 1 **teaspoon ground cinnamon**
 2 **apples, cored, peeled and chopped (about 2 cups)**
   Glaze (recipe follows)

1. Preheat oven to 350°F. Grease 13×9-inch baking pan. Combine flour, graham cracker crumbs, ½ cup brown sugar, butter, granulated sugar and cinnamon in large bowl until well blended. Reserve 1 cup crumb mixture. Press remaining crumb mixture onto bottom of prepared pan. Bake 8 minutes. Remove from oven; set aside.

2. Toss remaining ¼ cup brown sugar with apples in medium bowl until sugar is dissolved; spoon apples over baked crust. Sprinkle reserved 1 cup crumb mixture over filling. Bake 30 to 35 minutes or until apples are tender. Remove pan to wire rack; cool completely. Drizzle with Glaze; let stand until set. Cut into bars.   *Makes 3 dozen bars*

Glaze: Combine ½ cup powdered sugar and 1 tablespoon milk in small bowl until well blended.

*Clockwise from top left: Cinnamony Apple
Streusel Bars, Chocolate Cherry Bars (page 123),
Almond-Orange Shortbread (page 109) and
German Honey Bars (page 122)*

Cran-Raspberry Bars

2 cups all-purpose flour, divided
⅔ cup powdered sugar, divided
½ teaspoon salt, divided
¾ cup (1½ sticks) cold butter, cut into slices and divided
1 egg, separated
1 cup seedless red raspberry jam
1 cup coarsely chopped fresh or thawed frozen cranberries
   (about 1¼ cups whole cranberries)
½ cup coarsely chopped walnuts
2 tablespoons milk

1. Preheat oven to 350°F. Grease 9-inch square baking pan.

2. For crust, combine 1 cup flour, ⅓ cup powdered sugar and ¼ teaspoon salt in bowl of food processor fitted with steel blade; pulse to mix. Add ½ cup butter; process using on/off pulses until mixture resembles coarse crumbs. Press onto bottom and ½ inch up sides of prepared pan; brush with egg white. Bake about 20 minutes or until crust is golden and beginning to pull away from sides of pan.

3. Meanwhile, combine jam and cranberries in medium bowl; stir until blended. Spread jam mixture over baked crust; set aside.

4. For topping, combine remaining 1 cup flour, ⅓ cup powdered sugar and ¼ teaspoon salt in bowl of food processor fitted with steel blade; pulse to mix. Add remaining ¼ cup butter; process using on/off pulses until mixture resembles coarse crumbs. Stir in walnuts. Add egg yolk and milk; process using on/off pulses until mixture forms marble-sized chunks. Sprinkle topping over filling.

5. Bake about 30 minutes or until topping is golden and filling is bubbly. Cool completely on wire rack. Cut into bars. *Makes 16 bars*

Cran-Raspberry Bars

Pumpkin Cheesecake Squares

1½ cups gingersnap crumbs, plus additional for garnish
6 tablespoons butter, melted
2 eggs
¼ cup plus 2 tablespoons sugar, divided
2½ teaspoons vanilla, divided
1 package (8 ounces) plus 1 package (3 ounces) cream cheese, softened
1¼ cups solid-pack pumpkin
1 teaspoon ground cinnamon
¼ teaspoon ground ginger
¼ teaspoon ground nutmeg
¼ teaspoon ground cloves
1 cup sour cream

1. Preheat oven to 325°F. Lightly grease 13×9-inch baking pan. Combine 1½ cups crumbs and butter in small bowl. Press onto bottom of prepared pan. Bake 10 minutes.

2. Meanwhile, combine eggs, ¼ cup sugar and 1½ teaspoons vanilla in blender or food processor. Process about 1 minute or until smooth. Add cream cheese and pumpkin; process until well blended. Stir in cinnamon, ginger, nutmeg and cloves. Pour mixture evenly over hot crust. Bake 40 minutes.

3. For topping, whisk sour cream, remaining 2 tablespoons sugar and 1 teaspoon vanilla in small bowl until blended. Remove cheesecake from oven; spread sour cream mixture evenly over top. Bake 5 minutes. Turn oven off; open door halfway and let cheesecake cool in oven. When cool, refrigerate 2 hours. Garnish with gingersnap crumbs; cut into squares.

Makes about 3 dozen squares

Pumpkin Cheesecake Squares

Danish Raspberry Ribbons

1 cup (2 sticks) butter, softened
½ cup granulated sugar
1 egg
2 tablespoons milk
2 teaspoons vanilla
¼ teaspoon almond extract
2⅔ cups all-purpose flour
6 tablespoons seedless raspberry jam
Glaze (recipe follows)

1. Beat butter and sugar in large bowl with electric mixer at medium speed until light and fluffy. Beat in egg, milk, vanilla and almond extract until well blended.

2. Gradually add 1½ cups flour, beating at low speed until well blended. Stir in enough remaining flour to form stiff dough. Shape dough into disc. Wrap in plastic wrap; refrigerate until firm, at least 30 minutes or overnight.

3. Preheat oven to 375°F. Divide dough into 6 equal pieces. With floured hands, shape one dough piece at a time into ¾-inch-thick rope about 12 inches long. (Keep remaining dough pieces wrapped in refrigerator.) Place ropes 2 inches apart on ungreased cookie sheets.

4. Make ¼-inch-deep groove down center of each rope with handle of wooden spoon or finger. Bake 12 minutes. (Ropes will flatten to ½-inch-thick strips.) Remove from oven; spoon 1 tablespoon jam into each groove. Return to oven; bake 5 to 7 minutes or until strips are light golden brown. Cool strips 15 minutes on cookie sheet.

5. Prepare Glaze; drizzle over strips. Let stand 5 minutes to set. Cut cookie strips at 45° angle into 1-inch slices. Place cookies on wire racks; cool completely. *Makes 6 dozen cookies*

Glaze: Combine ½ cup powdered sugar, 1 tablespoon milk and 1 teaspoon vanilla in small bowl until well blended.

Holiday Walnut Berry Bites

MAZOLA® No Stick Cooking Spray
2½ cups all-purpose flour
1 cup cold margarine, cut into pieces
½ cup confectioners' sugar
½ teaspoon salt
1⅓ cups KARO® Light Corn Syrup
4 eggs
1 cup sugar
3 tablespoons butter, melted
2 cups fresh or thawed frozen cranberries, coarsely chopped
1 cup walnuts, chopped
1 cup white chocolate chips

Preheat oven to 350°F. Spray 15×10×1-inch baking pan with cooking spray. In a large bowl, beat flour, margarine, confectioners' sugar and salt at medium speed until mixture resembles coarse crumbs; press firmly and evenly into pan. Bake 20 minutes or until golden brown.

In a large bowl, beat Karo, eggs, sugar and butter until well blended. Stir in the cranberries and walnuts.

Spread mixture evenly over hot crust. Sprinkle white chocolate chips over the top. Bake 25 to 30 minutes or until set. Cool completely on a wire rack before cutting into bars. *Makes 4 dozen bars*

Prep Time: 30 minutes
Bake Time: 50 minutes

Helpful Hint

For a fancier appearance and more variety on your holiday cookie plate, try cutting bar cookies into diamonds. First, cut straight lines 1 to 1½ inches apart lengthwise, then cut straight lines 1½ inches apart diagonally.

Brownie Spice Squares

¾ cup (1½ sticks) butter, cut into chunks
4 squares (1 ounce each) unsweetened chocolate
3 eggs
1 cup granulated sugar
½ cup packed light brown sugar
¾ cup all-purpose flour
½ teaspoon ground cinnamon
¼ teaspoon salt
    Latte Glaze (recipe follows)
    Chocolate Curls (recipe follows, optional)

1. Preheat oven to 350°F. Grease 9-inch square baking pan. Place butter and chocolate in medium microwavable bowl. Microwave on HIGH 30 seconds; stir. Repeat as necessary until chocolate is melted and mixture is smooth. Let cool slightly.

2. Beat eggs in large bowl with electric mixer at medium speed until foamy. Add granulated sugar and brown sugar; beat until well blended and slightly thickened. Add flour, cinnamon and salt; stir until blended. Stir in chocolate mixture until well blended.

3. Spread batter in prepared pan. Bake 25 to 30 minutes or until edges are dry but center is still moist. Cool completely on wire rack.

4. Prepare Latte Glaze; spread over cooled brownies. Refrigerate at least 1 hour or until glaze is set. Cut into squares. Garnish with Chocolate Curls.

Makes 16 squares

Latte Glaze: Combine ¼ cup whipping cream, 1 teaspoon instant coffee granules, ⅛ teaspoon salt and ⅛ teaspoon ground cinnamon in small bowl; stir until coffee is dissolved. Gradually stir in 1 cup powdered sugar. Add additional cream, 1 tablespoon at a time, until of spreading consistency.

Chocolate Curls: Place 1-ounce square semisweet chocolate on small microwavable plate; microwave on HIGH 5 to 10 seconds. (Chocolate should still be firm.) Pull vegetable peeler across chocolate square to create curls. Place curls on waxed paper-lined baking sheet; refrigerate 15 minutes or until firm.

Brownie Spice Squares

Pumpkin Streusel Bars

1 cup granulated sugar
1 cup solid-pack pumpkin
½ cup vegetable oil
2 eggs
2 tablespoons butter, melted
1½ cups all-purpose flour, divided
1½ teaspoons baking powder
1 teaspoon ground cinnamon
¼ teaspoon salt
¼ teaspoon baking soda
⅛ teaspoon ground ginger
½ cup packed light brown sugar
¼ cup (½ stick) butter, cut into small pieces
1 cup coarsely chopped pecans

1. Preheat oven to 350°F. Grease 13×9-inch baking pan.

2. For bars, beat granulated sugar, pumpkin, oil, eggs and melted butter in large bowl with electric mixer at medium speed until well blended. Combine 1 cup flour, baking powder, cinnamon, salt, baking soda and ginger. Gradually add flour mixture to pumpkin mixture, beating after each addition. Spread batter in prepared pan.

3. For streusel, combine remaining ½ cup flour and brown sugar in large bowl. Cut ¼ cup butter into sugar mixture with pastry blender or two knives until mixture resembles coarse crumbs. Stir in pecans. Sprinkle streusel evenly over batter.

4. Bake about 35 minutes or until toothpick inserted into center comes out clean. Cool completely on wire rack. Cut into 3×1-inch bars.

Makes about 3 dozen bars

Pumpkin Streusel Bars

Fruitcake Bars

1 cup diced dried apricots
1 cup diced pitted dates
2 tablespoons rum or orange juice
1 cup packed dark brown sugar
½ cup (1 stick) butter, softened
3 eggs
   Freshly grated peel of 1 orange
1 teaspoon vanilla
1 cup all-purpose flour
¼ teaspoon salt
1½ cups chopped pecans, toasted*
1 cup semisweet chocolate chips
¾ cup white chocolate chips

*To toast pecans, spread in single layer on baking sheet. Bake in preheated 350°F oven 8 to 10 minutes or until golden brown, stirring frequently.

1. Grease 13×9-inch baking pan. Combine apricots, dates and rum in small bowl; let stand 30 minutes, stirring occasionally.

2. Preheat oven to 325°F. Beat brown sugar and butter in large bowl with electric mixer at medium speed until well blended. Add eggs, one at a time, beating after each addition. Add orange peel and vanilla; beat until blended. Add flour and salt; beat until blended. Stir in dried fruit, pecans and semisweet chocolate chips.

3. Spread batter in prepared pan. Bake about 35 minutes or until toothpick inserted into center comes out clean and edges begin to pull away from sides of pan. Sprinkle with white chocolate chips; let stand until chips are spreadable. Spread chips gently over top. Cool completely on wire rack. Cut into bars.   *Makes about 2½ dozen bars*

Fruitcake Bars

Sour Cream Brownies

Brownies
- 1 cup water
- 1 cup butter
- 3 tablespoons unsweetened cocoa powder
- 2 cups all-purpose flour
- 2 cups granulated sugar
- 1 teaspoon baking soda
- ½ teaspoon salt
- 1 (8-ounce) container dairy sour cream
- 2 eggs

Frosting
- 4 cups sifted powdered sugar
- 3 tablespoons unsweetened cocoa powder
- ½ cup butter, softened
- 6 tablespoons milk
- 1 cup chopped nuts

For brownies, preheat oven to 350°F. Grease 15×10×1-inch baking pan; set aside. Combine water, butter and cocoa in medium saucepan. Cook, stirring constantly, until mixture comes to a boil. Remove from heat; set aside. Combine flour, granulated sugar, baking soda and salt in medium bowl; set aside.

Beat sour cream and eggs at medium speed of electric mixer. Gradually add hot cocoa mixture, beating well. Blend in flour mixture; beat until smooth. Pour batter into prepared pan. Bake 25 to 30 minutes or until brownies spring back when lightly touched. Cool completely in pan on wire rack.

For frosting, combine powdered sugar and cocoa in large bowl; set aside. Beat butter in medium bowl at medium speed of electric mixer until creamy. Add powdered sugar mixture alternately with milk, beating well after each addition. Spread over cooled brownies. Sprinkle nuts over frosting.

Makes about 40 brownies

Favorite recipe from **Wisconsin Milk Marketing Board**

Almond-Orange Shortbread

1 cup (4 ounces) sliced almonds, divided
2 cups all-purpose flour
1 cup (2 sticks) cold butter, cut into pieces
½ cup sugar
½ cup cornstarch
2 tablespoons freshly grated orange peel
1 teaspoon almond extract

1. Preheat oven to 350°F. Spread ¾ cup almonds in single layer on cookie sheet. Bake 6 minutes or until golden brown, stirring frequently. Cool completely in pan. *Reduce oven temperature to 325°F.*

2. Place toasted almonds in food processor. Process using on/off pulses until almonds are coarsely chopped.

3. Add flour, butter, sugar, cornstarch, orange peel and almond extract to food processor. Process using on/off pulses until mixture resembles coarse crumbs.

4. Press dough firmly and evenly into 10×8¾-inch rectangle on large ungreased cookie sheet. Score dough into 1¼-inch squares. Press one slice of remaining almonds into center of each square.

5. Bake 30 to 40 minutes or until shortbread is lightly browned and firm. Immediately cut into squares along score lines with sharp knife. Remove cookies to wire racks; cool completely.   *Makes about 4½ dozen cookies*

Chewy Peanut Butter Brownies

¾ cup (1½ sticks) butter, melted
¾ cup creamy peanut butter
1¾ cups sugar
2 teaspoons vanilla
4 eggs
1¼ cups all-purpose flour
½ teaspoon baking powder
¼ teaspoon salt
¼ cup unsweetened cocoa powder

1. Preheat oven to 350°F. Grease 13×9-inch baking pan.

2. Beat butter and peanut butter in large bowl until well blended. Add sugar and vanilla; beat until blended. Add eggs; beat until well blended. Stir in flour, baking powder and salt just until blended. Reserve 1¾ cups batter. Stir cocoa into remaining batter.

3. Spread cocoa batter evenly in prepared pan. Top with reserved batter. Bake 30 minutes or until edges begin to pull away from sides of pan. Cool completely in pan on wire rack; cut into bars.   *Makes 3 dozen brownies*

Helpful Hint

Lightly coat your measuring cup with nonstick cooking spray before measuring sticky ingredients such as peanut butter, corn syrup, or molasses. That way it will slide out of the cup easily instead of clinging to the side.

Chewy Peanut Butter Brownies

Santa's Favorite Brownies

 1 cup (6 ounces) milk chocolate chips
 ½ cup (1 stick) butter
 ¾ cup granulated sugar
 2 eggs
 1 teaspoon vanilla
 1¼ cups all-purpose flour
 3 tablespoons unsweetened cocoa powder
 1 teaspoon baking powder
 ½ teaspoon salt
 ½ cup chopped walnuts
    Buttercream Frosting (recipe follows)
    Sprinkles and/or holiday decors (optional)

1. Preheat oven to 350°F. Grease 9-inch square baking pan.

2. Melt chocolate chips and butter with granulated sugar in medium saucepan over low heat, stirring constantly. Pour into large bowl.

3. Add eggs and vanilla. Beat with electric mixer at medium speed until well blended. Stir in flour, cocoa, baking powder and salt; blend well. Fold in walnuts. Spread in prepared pan.

4. Bake 25 to 30 minutes or until toothpick inserted into center comes out clean. Place pan on wire rack; cool completely.

5. Frost with Buttercream Frosting. Decorate with sprinkles, if desired.

Makes 16 brownies

Buttercream Frosting

 3 cups powdered sugar, sifted
 ½ cup (1 stick) butter, softened
 3 to 4 tablespoons milk, divided
 ½ teaspoon vanilla

Combine powdered sugar, butter, 2 tablespoons milk and vanilla in large bowl. Beat with electric mixer at low speed until blended. Beat at high speed until light and fluffy, adding more milk, 1 teaspoon at a time, as needed to reach spreading consistency. *Makes about 1½ cups frosting*

Santa's Favorite Brownies

Gingerbread Cheesecake Bars

  1 package (8 ounces) cream cheese, softened
⅔ cup granulated sugar, divided
  3 eggs
½ teaspoon vanilla
1½ teaspoons ground ginger, divided
½ cup (1 stick) butter, softened
¾ cup molasses
  2 cups all-purpose flour
  1 teaspoon baking soda
¾ teaspoon ground cinnamon
¼ teaspoon salt
¼ teaspoon ground allspice

1. Preheat oven to 350°F. Grease 13×9-inch baking pan.

2. Beat cream cheese and ⅓ cup sugar in medium bowl with electric mixer at medium speed until light and fluffy. Add 1 egg, vanilla and ½ teaspoon ginger; beat until well blended and smooth. Refrigerate until ready to use.

3. Beat butter and remaining ⅓ cup sugar in large bowl at medium speed until light and fluffy. Add molasses and remaining 2 eggs; beat until well blended. Combine flour, baking soda, remaining 1 teaspoon ginger, cinnamon, salt and allspice in medium bowl. Add flour mixture to butter mixture; beat just until blended. Spread batter evenly in prepared pan.

4. Drop cream cheese mixture by spoonfuls onto gingerbread batter; swirl with knife. Bake 25 to 30 minutes or until toothpick inserted into center comes out clean. Cool completely on wire rack.   *Makes 2 dozen bars*

Gingerbread Cheesecake Bars

Caramel Fudge Brownies

1 jar (12 ounces) caramel ice cream topping
1¼ cups all-purpose flour, divided
¼ teaspoon baking powder
  Dash salt
¾ cup (1½ sticks) butter
4 squares (1 ounce each) unsweetened chocolate, coarsely chopped
2 cups sugar
3 eggs
2 teaspoons vanilla
¾ cup semisweet chocolate chips
¾ cup chopped pecans

1. Preheat oven to 350°F. Lightly grease 13×9-inch baking pan.

2. Combine caramel topping and ¼ cup flour in small bowl; set aside. Combine remaining 1 cup flour, baking powder and salt in small bowl; mix well.

3. Place butter and unsweetened chocolate in large microwavable bowl. Microwave on HIGH 2 minutes or until butter is melted; stir until chocolate is completely melted.

4. Stir sugar into chocolate mixture. Add eggs and vanilla; stir until blended. Add flour mixture; stir until well blended. Spread batter evenly in prepared pan.

5. Bake 25 minutes. Remove brownies from oven; immediately spread caramel mixture over brownies. Sprinkle top evenly with chocolate chips and pecans.

6. Return pan to oven; bake about 22 minutes or until topping is bubbly. *Do not overbake.* Cool brownies completely in pan on wire rack. Cut into 2×1½-inch bars. *Makes 3 dozen brownies*

Orange-Cranberry Bars

½ cup dried cranberries
2 tablespoons frozen orange juice concentrate, thawed
1 cup sugar
½ cup unsweetened cocoa powder
½ cup (1 stick) butter, melted
2 eggs
2 teaspoons *each* freshly grated orange peel and vanilla
¾ cup all-purpose flour
½ teaspoon baking powder
¼ teaspoon salt
½ cup *each* white chocolate chips and chopped pecans

Preheat oven to 350°F. Grease 9×9-inch baking pan. Place cranberries and juice concentrate in microwavable bowl. Microwave on HIGH 30 seconds; stand, covered, 5 minutes. Beat sugar, cocoa and butter in medium bowl. Add eggs, orange peel and vanilla; beat until well blended. Stir in flour, baking powder and salt just until blended. Stir in cranberry mixture. Spread batter in prepared pan. Sprinkle with chocolate chips and pecans. Bake 30 minutes or until toothpick inserted into center comes out clean.   *Makes 16 bars*

Chewy Butterscotch Brownies

2½ cups all-purpose flour
1 teaspoon baking powder
½ teaspoon salt
1 cup (2 sticks) butter or margarine, softened
1¾ cups packed brown sugar
1 tablespoon vanilla extract
2 large eggs
1⅔ cups (11-ounce package) NESTLÉ® TOLL HOUSE® Butterscotch
   Flavored Morsels, *divided*
1 cup chopped nuts

PREHEAT oven to 350°F.

COMBINE flour, baking powder and salt in medium bowl. Beat butter, sugar and vanilla extract in large mixer bowl until creamy. Beat in eggs. Gradually beat in flour mixture. Stir in *1 cup* morsels and nuts. Spread into ungreased 13×9-inch baking pan. Sprinkle with *remaining* morsels.

BAKE for 30 to 40 minutes or until wooden pick inserted in center comes out clean. Cool in pan on wire rack.   *Makes about 4 dozen brownies*

Intense Mint Chocolate Brownies

Brownies
- 1 cup (2 sticks) butter
- 4 squares (1 ounce each) unsweetened chocolate
- 1½ cups granulated sugar
- 3 eggs
- ½ teaspoon salt
- ½ teaspoon mint extract
- ½ teaspoon vanilla
- ¾ cup all-purpose flour

Mint Frosting
- 6 tablespoons butter, softened
- ½ teaspoon mint extract
- 2 to 3 drops green food coloring
- 2 cups powdered sugar
- 2 to 3 tablespoons milk

Chocolate Glaze
- ⅓ cup semisweet chocolate chips
- 2 tablespoons butter

1. Preheat oven to 325°F. Grease and flour 9-inch square baking pan.

2. For brownies, melt butter and chocolate in top of double boiler over simmering water. Remove from heat. Beat in granulated sugar, eggs, salt, mint extract and vanilla until well blended. Stir in flour. Spread batter in prepared pan. Bake 35 minutes or until top is firm and edges begin to pull away from sides of pan. Cool completely in pan on wire rack.

3. For mint frosting, beat butter, mint extract and food coloring in large bowl with electric mixer at medium speed until fluffy. Add powdered sugar, ½ cup at a time, beating well after each addition. Beat in milk, one tablespoon at a time, until spreading consistency is reached. Spread frosting over cooled brownies.

4. For chocolate glaze, place chocolate chips and butter in microwavable bowl. Microwave on LOW (30%) 1 minute; stir. Repeat until chocolate chips are melted and mixture is smooth. Drizzle glaze over frosting. Let stand 30 minutes or until glaze is set.   *Makes about 2 dozen brownies*

Intense Mint Chocolate Brownies

Primo Pumpkin Brownies

¾ cup packed brown sugar
½ cup (1 stick) butter, softened
1 teaspoon vanilla
1 egg
1⅓ cups all-purpose flour
1 cup solid-pack pumpkin
2 teaspoons pumpkin pie spice*
1 teaspoon baking powder
¼ teaspoon salt
½ cup toffee baking bits
    White Chocolate Cream Cheese Frosting (recipe follows)

Substitute 1 teaspoon ground cinnamon, ½ teaspoon ground ginger and ¼ teaspoon each ground allspice and ground nutmeg for 2 teaspoons pumpkin pie spice.

1. Preheat oven to 350°F. Grease 8-inch square baking pan. Beat brown sugar, butter and vanilla in large bowl with electric mixer at medium speed until smooth. Add egg; beat until fluffy. Stir in flour, pumpkin, pumpkin pie spice, baking powder and salt. Fold in toffee bits. Spread evenly in prepared pan.

2. Bake 40 to 45 minutes or until toothpick inserted near center comes out clean. Cool completely in pan on wire rack.

3. Prepare White Chocolate Cream Cheese Frosting. Frost brownies; cut into squares. *Makes 9 brownies*

White Chocolate Cream Cheese Frosting

2 tablespoons whipping cream
4 squares (1 ounce each) white chocolate, chopped
6 ounces cream cheese, softened
⅓ cup powdered sugar, sifted

1. Heat cream in saucepan over medium heat until almost boiling; remove from heat. Add white chocolate; stir until completely melted. Cool slightly.

2. Beat cream cheese and sugar in large bowl with electric mixer at medium speed 1 minute or until fluffy. Beat in chocolate mixture until smooth.
Makes about 2 cups frosting

Primo Pumpkin Brownie

German Honey Bars

2¾ cups all-purpose flour
2 teaspoons ground cinnamon
1 teaspoon baking powder
½ teaspoon baking soda
½ teaspoon salt
½ teaspoon ground cardamom
½ teaspoon ground ginger
½ cup honey
½ cup dark molasses
3 tablespoons butter
¾ cup packed brown sugar
1 egg
½ cup chopped toasted almonds (optional)
Lemon Glaze (recipe follows)

1. Preheat oven to 350°F. Grease 15×10×1-inch jelly-roll pan. Combine flour, cinnamon, baking powder, baking soda, salt, cardamom and ginger in medium bowl. Combine honey and molasses in medium saucepan; bring to a boil over medium heat. Remove from heat. Add butter; stir until melted. Cool 10 minutes. Stir in brown sugar and egg.

2. Place brown sugar mixture in large bowl. Gradually add flour mixture, beating with electric mixer at low speed until dough forms. Stir in almonds. (Dough will be slightly sticky.) Spread dough evenly in prepared pan. Bake 20 to 22 minutes or until golden brown and set. Remove pan to wire rack; cool completely.

3. Prepare Lemon Glaze. Spread over cooled bars. Let stand until set, about 30 minutes. Cut into 2×1-inch bars.   *Makes about 6 dozen bars*

Lemon Glaze: Combine 1¼ cups powdered sugar, 1 teaspoon freshly grated lemon peel and 3 tablespoons lemon juice in medium bowl until well blended.

Chocolate Cherry Bars

1 cup (2 sticks) butter or margarine
¾ cup HERSHEY'S Cocoa or HERSHEY'S SPECIAL DARK™ Cocoa
2 cups sugar
4 eggs
1½ cups plus ⅓ cup all-purpose flour, divided
⅓ cup chopped almonds
1 can (14 ounces) sweetened condensed milk (not evaporated milk)
½ teaspoon almond extract
1 cup HERSHEY'S MINI KISSES® Brand Milk Chocolates
1 cup chopped maraschino cherries, drained

1. Heat oven to 350°F. Generously grease 13×9×2-inch baking pan.

2. Melt butter in large saucepan over low heat; stir in cocoa until smooth. Remove from heat. Add sugar, 3 eggs, 1½ cups flour and almonds; mix well. Pour into prepared pan. Bake 20 minutes.

3. Meanwhile, whisk together remaining 1 egg, remaining ⅓ cup flour, sweetened condensed milk and almond extract. Pour over baked layer; sprinkle chocolate pieces and cherries over top. Return to oven.

4. Bake additional 20 to 25 minutes or until set and edges are golden brown. Cool completely in pan on wire rack. Refrigerate until cold, 6 hours or overnight. Cut into bars. Cover; refrigerate leftover bars.

Makes about 48 bars

Helpful Hint

For easy removal of brownies and bar cookies with no cleanup, line the baking pan with foil and leave at least 3 inches hanging over each end. Use the foil to lift out the treats, place them on a cutting board and remove the foil. Then simply cut them into pieces.

Elegant Yuletide Treasures

Pink Peppermint Meringues

　3 egg whites
⅛ teaspoon peppermint extract
　5 drops red food coloring
½ cup superfine sugar*
　6 peppermint candies, finely crushed

*Or use ½ cup granulated sugar processed in food processor until very fine.

1. Preheat oven to 200°F. Line 2 cookie sheets with parchment paper.

2. Beat egg whites in medium bowl with electric mixer at medium-high speed about 45 seconds or until frothy. Beat in extract and food coloring. Add sugar, 1 tablespoon at a time, while mixer is running, beating until egg whites are stiff and glossy.

3. Drop meringue by teaspoonfuls into 1-inch mounds on prepared cookie sheets; sprinkle evenly with crushed candies.

4. Bake 2 hours or until meringues are dry when tapped. Transfer parchment paper with meringues to wire racks to cool completely.

Makes about 6 dozen meringues

Clockwise from top left: Pink Peppermint Meringues, Pistachio Cookie Cups (page 131), Candy Cane Biscotti (page 130) and Eggnog Cream Cups (page 134)

Brandy Snaps with Lemon Ricotta Cream

Cookies
>   ½ cup (1 stick) butter
>   ½ cup sugar
>   ⅓ cup light corn syrup
>   1 cup all-purpose flour
>   1 tablespoon brandy or cognac

Filling
>   ½ cup (1 stick) butter, softened
>   ½ cup ricotta cheese
>   ¼ cup sugar
>   2 teaspoons freshly grated lemon peel
>   1 tablespoon fresh lemon juice

1. Preheat oven to 325°F. For cookies, place butter, sugar and corn syrup in medium saucepan over medium heat; cook and stir until butter is melted and mixture is blended. Stir in flour and brandy.

2. Drop level tablespoonfuls of batter about 3 inches apart onto ungreased cookie sheet, spacing to fit 4 cookies on sheet. Bake one cookie sheet at a time about 12 minutes or until golden brown.

3. When just cool enough to handle, usually within 1 minute, remove each cookie from baking sheet and quickly wrap around wooden spoon handle to form tube. (If cookies become too firm to wrap, return to oven 10 to 15 seconds to soften.)

4. For filling, process butter, ricotta, sugar, lemon peel and lemon juice in food processor until smooth.

5. Place filling in pastry bag fitted with plain or star tip, or in 1-quart food storage bag with small piece of corner cut off. Fill cookies just before serving. *Makes 2 dozen cookies*

Brandy Snaps with Lemon Ricotta Cream

Browned Butter Spritz Cookies

1½ cups (3 sticks) butter
½ cup granulated sugar
¼ cup powdered sugar
1 egg yolk
1 teaspoon vanilla
⅛ teaspoon almond extract
2½ cups all-purpose flour
¼ cup cake flour
¼ teaspoon salt

1. Melt butter in medium heavy saucepan over medium heat until amber in color, stirring frequently. Transfer butter to large bowl. Cover and refrigerate about 2 hours or until solid. Let butter stand at room temperature about 15 minutes to soften before completing recipe.

2. Preheat oven to 350°F. Beat browned butter, granulated sugar and powdered sugar in large bowl with electric mixer at medium speed until light and fluffy. Add egg yolk, vanilla and almond extract; beat until well blended.

3. Combine all-purpose flour, cake flour and salt in small bowl. Add flour mixture to butter mixture; beat until well blended.

4. Fit cookie press with desired plate. Fill press with dough; press dough 1 inch apart on ungreased cookie sheets. Bake 10 to 12 minutes or until lightly browned. Cool 5 minutes on cookie sheets; transfer to wire racks to cool completely. *Makes about 8 dozen cookies*

 ### Helpful Hint

To add holiday sparkle to these delicious cookies, before baking, sprinkle them with red or green decorating sugar. For pretty trees or wreaths, tint the dough with green food coloring before pressing. Sprinkle with colored nonpareils as ornaments before baking, or pipe red icing bows on the baked and cooled cookies.

Browned Butter Spritz Cookies

Candy Cane Biscotti

1 cup sugar
½ cup (1 stick) butter, softened
2 tablespoons water
2 eggs
1 teaspoon peppermint extract
3½ cups all-purpose flour
1 cup finely crushed peppermint candy canes, divided
½ cup slivered almonds, toasted*
1 teaspoon baking powder
½ teaspoon salt
4 squares (1 ounce each) white chocolate, melted

*To toast almonds, spread in single layer on cookie sheet. Bake in preheated 350°F oven 8 to 10 minutes or until golden brown, stirring frequently.

1. Preheat oven to 350°F. Line 2 cookie sheets with parchment paper.

2. Beat sugar, butter, water, eggs and extract in large bowl with electric mixer at medium speed until well blended. Add flour, ½ cup crushed candy canes, almonds, baking powder and salt. Beat at low speed just until blended.

3. Divide dough in half. Shape each half into 10×3-inch log; place each log on separate prepared cookie sheet. Bake 30 minutes or until center is firm to the touch. Let cool 15 to 20 minutes.

4. Cut logs diagonally into ½-inch slices with serrated knife. Place slices, cut sides down, on cookie sheets; bake 15 minutes. Turn slices over; bake 12 to 15 minutes or until edges are browned. Cool completely on wire racks.

5. Dip each cookie halfway in melted chocolate. Sprinkle cookies with remaining ½ cup crushed candy canes. *Makes 40 cookies*

Pistachio Cookie Cups

½ cup (1 stick) plus 1 tablespoon butter, softened and divided
1 package (3 ounces) cream cheese, softened
2 tablespoons granulated sugar
1 cup all-purpose flour
½ teaspoon freshly grated orange peel
1 cup powdered sugar
½ cup chopped pistachio nuts
⅓ cup dried cranberries
1 egg
½ teaspoon orange extract
    Additional powdered sugar (optional)

1. Beat ½ cup butter, cream cheese and granulated sugar in large bowl with electric mixer at medium speed until light and fluffy. Add flour and orange peel; beat just until blended. Shape into ball; wrap in plastic wrap. Freeze 30 minutes.

2. Combine powdered sugar, nuts, cranberries, egg, remaining 1 tablespoon butter and extract in medium bowl; mix well. Set aside.

3. Preheat oven to 350°F. Lightly grease 24 mini (1¾-inch) muffin cups.

4. Press 1 tablespoon dough firmly onto bottom and up side of each muffin cup. Fill shells three-fourths full with nut mixture.

5. Bake 25 minutes or until filling is set. Remove cookie cups to wire racks; cool completely. Sprinkle with powdered sugar.   *Makes 2 dozen cups*

Sparkling Snowflakes

½ **cup sugar**
¼ **cup (½ stick) butter, softened**
1 **egg**
   Freshly grated peel of 1 lemon
1¼ **cups all-purpose flour**
1 **teaspoon baking powder**
⅛ **teaspoon salt**
   White Glaze (recipe follows)
   Decorating sugar, edible glitter and dragées (optional)

1. Beat sugar and butter in large bowl with electric mixer at medium speed until well blended. Add egg and lemon peel; beat until well blended. Combine flour, baking powder and salt in medium bowl; gradually add to butter mixture, beating well after each addition. Shape dough into ball. (Dough will be sticky.) Wrap dough in plastic wrap; flatten into disc. Refrigerate 2 to 3 hours or until firm.

2. Preheat oven to 375°F. Line cookie sheets with parchment paper. Roll dough between floured sheets of parchment paper to ¼-inch thickness. Cut dough with floured 2½- to 5-inch snowflake cookie cutters. Place cutouts on prepared cookie sheets. Repeat with trimmings. Using tip of sharp knife, cut hole near top of each snowflake to allow for piece of ribbon to be inserted as hanger.

3. Bake 8 to 10 minutes or until firm but not browned. Cool on cookie sheets 1 minute. Remove to wire racks; cool completely.

4. Prepare White Glaze; spread on cookies. Place cookies on wire racks set over waxed paper; decorate as desired. Let cookies stand until glaze is set.

5. Pull ribbon through opening in top of each snowflake and tie small knot in ribbon ends.   *Makes 1½ to 2 dozen cookies*

White Glaze: Combine 4 cups powdered sugar, ¼ cup water and 3 tablespoons meringue powder in large bowl; beat with electric mixer at high speed for 6 to 7 minutes to make spreadable glaze. (Meringue powder is a dried egg white-based powder. It can be found in the cake decorating section of most craft stores.)

Sparkling Snowflakes

Eggnog Cream Cups

1 cup all-purpose flour
⅓ cup plus 3 tablespoons sugar, divided
¼ teaspoon salt
½ teaspoon ground nutmeg, divided, plus additional for garnish
½ cup (1 stick) butter, softened
¾ cup cold whipping cream
3 tablespoons egg substitute
¼ teaspoon rum extract

1. Lightly grease 24 mini (1¾-inch) muffin cups. Combine flour, ⅓ cup sugar, salt and ¼ teaspoon nutmeg in large bowl. Add butter; beat with electric mixer at medium speed until coarse crumbs form. Mix by hand until dough forms a ball. Shape dough into 24 (1-inch) balls; press onto bottoms and up sides of prepared muffin cups. Refrigerate 15 minutes.

2. Preheat oven to 350°F. Bake cups 13 to 15 minutes or until golden brown. Press down center of cups if necessary. Let cool in pans on wire racks 10 minutes. Remove from pans; cool completely.

3. Beat cream and remaining 3 tablespoons sugar in large bowl with electric mixer at high speed until soft peaks form. Add egg substitute, remaining ¼ teaspoon nutmeg and rum extract; beat until stiff peaks form. *Do not overbeat.* Refrigerate until ready to serve.

4. Just before serving, pipe or spoon about 1½ tablespoons cream mixture into each cooled cookie cup. Sprinkle with additional nutmeg.

Makes 2 dozen cups

Tip: Use the back of a melon baller to push the centers of the cookies down after baking.

Linzer Sandwich Cookies

1⅓ cups all-purpose flour
¼ teaspoon baking powder
¼ teaspoon salt
¾ cup granulated sugar
½ cup (1 stick) butter, softened
1 egg
1 teaspoon vanilla
Powdered sugar (optional)
Seedless red raspberry jam

1. Combine flour, baking powder and salt in small bowl. Beat granulated sugar and butter in medium bowl with electric mixer at medium speed until light and fluffy. Beat in egg and vanilla. Gradually add flour mixture, beating at low speed until dough forms. Divide dough in half. Wrap each half in plastic wrap; refrigerate 2 hours or until firm.

2. Preheat oven to 375°F. Working with 1 portion at a time, roll dough on lightly floured surface to ³⁄₁₆-inch thickness. Cut dough with floured cookie cutters, cutting equal numbers of each shape. (If dough becomes too soft, refrigerate several minutes before continuing.) Cut 1-inch centers out of half the cutouts of each shape. Repeat with trimmings. Place cutouts 1½ to 2 inches apart on ungreased cookie sheets. Bake 7 to 9 minutes or until edges are lightly browned. Let cookies stand on cookie sheets 1 to 2 minutes. Remove cookies to wire racks to cool completely.

3. Sprinkle cookies with holes with powdered sugar, if desired. Spread jam on flat sides of whole cookies, spreading almost to edges. Place cookies with holes, flat sides down, over jam.

Makes about 2 dozen sandwich cookies

Pineapple-Coconut Crescents

2 cups all-purpose flour
¼ cup cornstarch
¼ teaspoon salt
1 cup (2 sticks) butter, softened
½ cup granulated sugar
1 teaspoon vanilla
¾ cup flaked coconut, toasted
½ cup drained crushed pineapple
  Powdered sugar

1. Sift flour, cornstarch and salt into medium bowl. Beat butter, granulated sugar and vanilla in large bowl until creamy. Gradually add flour mixture, beating until well blended. Stir in coconut and pineapple. *Do not overmix.* Refrigerate dough at least 1 hour or until firm.

2. Preheat oven to 325°F. Shape dough into crescents. Place 2 inches apart on ungreased cookie sheets. Bake 20 minutes or until golden brown. Let cool on cookie sheets 2 minutes. Transfer to wire racks; cool completely. Sprinkle with powdered sugar.   *Makes about 2½ dozen cookies*

Helpful Hint

To toast coconut, spread it out in an even layer on an ungreased cookie sheet. Bake in a preheated 350°F oven for 5 to 7 minutes, stirring occasionally, until the coconut is golden brown. Let it cool completely before using.

Pineapple-Coconut Crescents

Holiday Buttons

½ cup (1 stick) butter, softened
1¼ cups chocolate-hazelnut spread,* divided
⅓ cup granulated sugar
⅓ cup packed light brown sugar
1 egg
½ teaspoon almond extract
2 cups all-purpose flour
¼ teaspoon salt
⅛ teaspoon baking powder
Decors, nonpareils and decorating sugar

Can be found in most supermarkets near the peanut butter.

1. Beat butter, ½ cup chocolate-hazelnut spread, granulated sugar and brown sugar in large bowl with electric mixer at medium speed until well blended. Add egg and extract; beat until well blended. Combine flour, salt and baking powder; gradually add flour mixture to butter mixture, beating after each addition. Divide dough into four pieces; shape each piece into 7-inch-long log. Wrap in plastic wrap; refrigerate 2 to 3 hours or until firm.

2. Preheat oven to 325°F. Lightly grease cookie sheets or line with parchment paper. Cut dough into ⅜-inch-thick slices; place 1 inch apart on prepared cookie sheets. Poke 4 or 5 holes into slices with toothpick or straw.

3. Bake 12 to 14 minutes or until cookies are set. Cool on cookie sheets 1 minute. Remove to wire racks; cool completely.

4. Spread 1 teaspoon chocolate-hazelnut spread on flat sides of half of cookies; top with remaining cookies. Roll sides of sandwich cookies in decors.   *Makes 3½ dozen sandwich cookies*

Holiday Buttons

Mocha Crinkles

1⅓ cups packed light brown sugar
½ cup vegetable oil
¼ cup sour cream
1 egg
1 teaspoon vanilla
1¾ cups all-purpose flour
¾ cup unsweetened cocoa powder
2 teaspoons instant espresso powder or coffee granules
1 teaspoon baking soda
¼ teaspoon salt
⅛ teaspoon black pepper
½ cup powdered sugar

1. Beat brown sugar and oil in large bowl with electric mixer at medium speed until well blended. Add sour cream, egg and vanilla; beat until well blended.

2. Combine flour, cocoa, espresso powder, baking soda, salt and pepper in medium bowl. Add flour mixture to brown sugar mixture; beat until well blended. Cover dough; refrigerate 3 to 4 hours or until firm.

3. Preheat oven to 350°F. Place powdered sugar in shallow bowl. Shape dough into 1-inch balls. Roll balls in powdered sugar; place 2 inches apart on ungreased cookie sheets.

4. Bake 10 to 12 minutes or until tops of cookies are firm. *Do not overbake.* Remove to wire racks to cool completely.

Makes about 6 dozen cookies

Butterscotch Almond Crescents

1 cup (2 sticks) butter, softened
½ cup plus 1 tablespoon powdered sugar
¼ teaspoon salt
1 teaspoon almond extract
1¾ cups all-purpose flour
¾ cup ground almonds
   Butterscotch Glaze (recipe follows)
½ cup sliced almonds

1. Preheat oven to 300°F. Line cookie sheets with parchment paper.

2. Beat butter, sugar and salt in large bowl with electric mixer at medium speed until light and fluffy. Add extract; beat until well blended. Gradually add flour, beating until well blended. Stir in ground almonds until well blended.

3. Shape dough by tablespoonfuls into 3-inch crescents; place on prepared cookie sheets. Bake 20 to 25 minutes or until lightly browned. Cool 5 minutes on cookie sheets; transfer to wire racks to cool completely.

4. Prepare Butterscotch Glaze; drizzle over crescents. Sprinkle with sliced almonds; let stand 30 minutes or until glaze is set.

Makes about 3 dozen cookies

Butterscotch Glaze

½ cup packed light brown sugar
2 tablespoons half-and-half
1½ tablespoons butter
¼ teaspoon salt

Combine brown sugar, half-and-half, butter and salt in small saucepan. Cook over low heat, stirring constantly, until butter melts and sugar dissolves.

Makes about ½ cup glaze

Holiday Triple Chocolate Yule Logs

1¾ **cups all-purpose flour**
¾ **cup powdered sugar**
¼ **cup unsweetened cocoa powder**
⅛ **teaspoon salt**
1 **cup (2 sticks) butter, softened**
1 **teaspoon vanilla**
1 **cup white chocolate chips**
  Chocolate sprinkles

1. Combine flour, powdered sugar, cocoa and salt in medium bowl. Beat butter and vanilla in large bowl with electric mixer at medium-low speed until fluffy. Gradually beat in flour mixture until well blended. Wrap dough in plastic wrap; refrigerate at least 30 minutes.

2. Preheat oven to 350°F. Shape dough into 2-inch logs about ½ inch thick. Place 2 inches apart on ungreased cookie sheets.

3. Bake 12 minutes or until set. Let stand on cookie sheets 2 minutes. Transfer to wire racks; cool completely.

4. Place white chocolate chips in small microwavable bowl. Microwave on HIGH 45 seconds; stir until completely melted. Place chocolate sprinkles in another small bowl. Dip each end of cooled cookies first into white chocolate and then into chocolate sprinkles. Place on wire racks; let stand about 25 minutes or until set.   *Makes about 3 dozen cookies*

Cranberry Orange Crescents

1 cup (2 sticks) butter, softened
1 cup powdered sugar, divided
    Freshly grated peel of 1 large orange
3 tablespoons orange juice
2¼ cups all-purpose flour
¼ teaspoon salt
¼ teaspoon baking powder
1 cup chopped sweetened dried cranberries
1 cup pecan halves, toasted* and finely chopped

To toast pecans, spread in single layer on cookie sheet. Bake in preheated 350°F oven 8 to 10 minutes or until golden brown, stirring frequently.

1. Lightly grease cookie sheets or line with parchment paper.

2. Beat butter, ¾ cup powdered sugar, orange peel and juice in large bowl with electric mixer at medium speed until well blended. Combine flour, salt and baking powder in small bowl; gradually add to butter mixture, beating after each addition. Stir in cranberries and pecans.

3. Shape dough by rounded teaspoonfuls into 2-inch crescents; place 1 inch apart on prepared cookie sheets. Refrigerate 30 minutes.

4. Preheat oven to 350°F. Bake crescents 12 to 14 minutes or until edges are lightly browned. Remove to wire rack to cool slightly. Sprinkle remaining ¼ cup powdered sugar over warm cookies.

Makes about 6 dozen cookies

Cranberry Orange Crescents

Brown Sugar Shortbread

1 cup (2 sticks) I CAN'T BELIEVE IT'S NOT BUTTER!® Spread
¾ cup firmly packed light brown sugar
2 cups all-purpose flour
⅓ cup semisweet chocolate chips, melted

Preheat oven to 325°F. Grease 9-inch round cake pan; set aside.

In large bowl, with electric mixer, beat I Can't Believe It's Not Butter!®
Spread and brown sugar until light and fluffy, about 5 minutes. Gradually
add flour and beat on low speed until blended. Spread mixture into prepared
pan and press into even layer. With knife, score surface into 16 pie-shaped
wedges.

Bake 45 minutes or until lightly golden. On wire rack, cool 20 minutes;
remove from pan and cool completely. Cut into wedges. To decorate, place
melted chocolate in small food storage bag. Snip off corner of bag; drizzle
chocolate over shortbread. *Makes 16 servings*

Decadent Coconut Macaroons

1 package (14 ounces) flaked coconut
¾ cup sugar
6 tablespoons all-purpose flour
¼ teaspoon salt
4 egg whites
1 teaspoon vanilla
1 cup (6 ounces) semisweet chocolate chips, melted

1. Preheat oven to 325°F. Line cookie sheets with parchment paper or grease
and dust with flour.

2. Combine coconut, sugar, flour and salt in large bowl; mix well. Beat in
egg whites and vanilla. Drop batter by tablespoonfuls 2 inches apart onto
prepared cookie sheets.

3. Bake 20 minutes or until cookies are set and light golden brown.
Immediately remove from cookie sheets to wire racks; cool completely.

4. Dip cooled cookies in melted chocolate; place on waxed-paper-lined
tray. Let stand at room temperature or until chocolate is set.
Makes about 3 dozen cookies

Brown Sugar Shortbread

Mint Chocolate Delights

Cookies
- ½ cup (1 stick) butter, softened
- ½ cup granulated sugar
- ⅓ cup packed light brown sugar
- ⅓ cup semisweet chocolate chips, melted
- 1 egg
- ½ teaspoon vanilla
- 1½ cups all-purpose flour
- ¼ cup unsweetened cocoa powder
- ¼ teaspoon salt

Mint Filling
- 2½ cups powdered sugar
- ½ cup (1 stick) butter, softened
- ¼ teaspoon salt
- ½ teaspoon mint extract
- 3 to 4 drops red food coloring
- 2 to 3 tablespoons milk or half-and-half

1. For cookies, beat butter and sugars in large bowl with electric mixer at medium speed until creamy. Add melted chocolate, egg and vanilla; beat until well blended. Combine flour, cocoa and salt in small bowl; gradually add to butter mixture, beating until well blended. Shape dough into 16-inch-long log. Wrap in plastic wrap; refrigerate about 1 hour or until firm.

2. Preheat oven to 400°F. Lightly grease cookie sheets or line with parchment paper. Cut log into ⅓-inch-thick slices; place on prepared cookie sheets. Bake 10 to 12 minutes or until set. Cool 5 minutes on cookie sheets. Remove to wire racks to cool completely.

3. For mint filling, combine powdered sugar, butter and salt in large bowl; beat until well blended. Add mint extract and food coloring; beat until well blended and evenly tinted. Add enough milk, 1 tablespoon at a time, to make filling fluffy. Spread or pipe filling on bottoms of half the cooled cookies. Top with remaining cookies.   *Makes 24 sandwich cookies*

Walnut Christmas Balls

1 cup California walnuts
⅔ cup powdered sugar, divided
1 cup butter or margarine, softened
1 teaspoon vanilla
1¾ cups all-purpose flour
Chocolate Filling (recipe follows)

In food processor or blender, process walnuts with 2 tablespoons of the sugar until finely ground; set aside. In large bowl, cream butter and remaining sugar. Beat in vanilla. Add flour and ¾ cup of the walnuts; mix until blended. Roll dough into about 3 dozen walnut-size balls. Place 2 inches apart on ungreased cookie sheets. Bake in preheated 350°F oven 10 to 12 minutes or until just golden around edges. Remove to wire racks to cool completely. Prepare Chocolate Filling. Place generous teaspoonful of filling on flat side of half the cookies. Top with remaining cookies, flat side down, forming sandwiches. Roll chocolate edges of cookies in remaining ground walnuts. *Makes about 1½ dozen sandwich cookies*

Chocolate Filling: Chop 3 squares (1 ounce each) semisweet chocolate into small pieces; place in food processor or blender with ½ teaspoon vanilla. In small saucepan, heat 2 tablespoons butter or margarine and 2 tablespoons whipping cream over medium heat until hot; pour over chocolate. Process until chocolate is melted, turning machine off and scraping sides as needed. With machine running, gradually add 1 cup powdered sugar; process until smooth.

Favorite recipe from **Walnut Marketing Board**

Truffle Brownie Bites

Brownies
- ⅔ **cup semisweet chocolate chips**
- ½ **cup (1 stick) butter, cut into chunks**
- 1⅓ **cups sugar**
- 3 **eggs**
- 1 **teaspoon vanilla**
- 1 **cup minus 2 tablespoons all-purpose flour**
- ¼ **teaspoon salt**

Ganache
- 7 **tablespoons whipping cream**
- ¾ **cup semisweet chocolate chips**
- **Holiday sprinkles**

1. Preheat oven to 350°F. Line 36 mini (1¾-inch) muffin cups with foil or paper baking cups; set aside.

2. For brownies, combine chocolate chips and butter in large microwavable bowl. Microwave on HIGH 30 seconds; stir. Repeat as necessary until chips are melted and mixture is smooth. Let cool slightly.

3. Add sugar to melted chocolate mixture; beat until well blended. Add eggs, one at a time, beating after each addition. Stir in vanilla. Add flour and salt; beat until well blended.

4. Spoon batter into prepared muffin cups, filling about three-fourths full. Bake 15 to 17 minutes or until tops are firm to the touch. *Do not overbake.* Cool 5 minutes in pans on wire racks. Remove from pans; cool completely.

5. For ganache, place cream in small saucepan over medium heat; bring to a simmer. Remove from heat; add ¾ cup chocolate chips. Stir until chips are melted and mixture is smooth. Let stand about 2 minutes to thicken and cool slightly.

6. Line cookie sheets with waxed paper; place brownies on prepared cookie sheets. Spread 1 teaspoon ganache over each brownie. Decorate with sprinkles. Refrigerate about 30 minutes or until ganache is set.

Makes 3 dozen bites

Truffle Brownie Bites

Eggnog Cookies

Cookies
   1 cup (2 sticks) butter, softened
   1¼ cups plus 1 tablespoon granulated sugar, divided
   1 egg yolk
   ½ cup sour cream
   2½ cups all-purpose flour
   ¼ teaspoon salt
   ½ teaspoon grated nutmeg
   ¼ teaspoon ground ginger

Filling
   ½ cup (1 stick) butter, softened
   ¼ cup shortening
   2½ cups powdered sugar
   2 tablespoons brandy or milk

1. Preheat oven to 350°F. Lightly grease cookie sheets.

2. For cookies, beat butter and 1¼ cups granulated sugar in large bowl with electric mixer at medium speed until light and fluffy. Add egg yolk; beat until blended. Add sour cream; beat until well blended. Combine flour and salt in small bowl; gradually add to butter mixture, beating until well blended.

3. Shape dough by rounded teaspoonfuls into balls. Place on prepared cookie sheets; flatten slightly. Combine remaining 1 tablespoon granulated sugar, nutmeg and ginger in small bowl; sprinkle over cookies.

4. Bake about 12 minutes or until edges are golden. Cool 5 minutes on cookie sheets. Remove to wire racks to cool completely.

5. For filling, beat butter and shortening in medium bowl until well blended. Add powdered sugar and brandy; beat until well blended. Spread or pipe filling on bottoms of half the cooled cookies. Top with remaining cookies.

Makes about 6 dozen sandwich cookies

Holiday Spice Prints

1 cup packed dark brown sugar
¾ cup (1½ sticks) butter, softened
1 egg
¼ cup molasses
1 teaspoon WATKINS® Vanilla
2½ cups all-purpose flour
2 teaspoons baking soda
2 teaspoons WATKINS® Ginger
1 teaspoon WATKINS® Ground Cinnamon
¾ teaspoon WATKINS® Ground Cloves
½ teaspoon WATKINS® Allspice
¼ teaspoon salt (optional)
  Granulated sugar

Beat brown sugar and butter in large bowl until creamy. Beat in egg, molasses and vanilla. Combine flour, baking soda, spices and salt, if desired. Stir into butter mixture until well blended. Chill dough for 1 hour.

Preheat oven to 375°F. Grease cookie sheets. Place granulated sugar in shallow bowl. Roll dough into 1½-inch balls; dip tops in granulated sugar. Place balls, sugar side up, about 3 inches apart on prepared cookie sheets. Bake for 10 to 12 minutes or until set but not hard. Firmly press top of each cookie with clay stamp or wooden butter mold immediately after removing from oven. Pierce top of each cookie with drinking straw to make hole for hanging, if desired. Transfer to wire racks to cool completely. When cool, thread each cookie with ribbon for hanging.

Makes 5 about dozen cookies

 **Helpful Hint**

Just for fun, host an old-fashioned cookie swap. Each guest brings a batch of his or her favorite cookies, enough for everyone to take some home. As the host, you provide containers for collecting and carrying all the cookies, as well as a beverage or two.

Acknowledgments

The publisher would like to thank the companies and organizations listed below for the use of their recipes and photographs in this publication.

ACH Food Companies, Inc.

Cherry Marketing Institute

Dole Food Company, Inc.

The Hershey Company

© Mars, Incorporated 2007

Nestlé USA

Sun•Maid® Growers of California

Unilever

Walnut Marketing Board

Watkins Incorporated

Wisconsin Milk Marketing Board

Index

Metric Conversion Chart

VOLUME MEASUREMENTS (dry)

1/8 teaspoon = 0.5 mL
1/4 teaspoon = 1 mL
1/2 teaspoon = 2 mL
3/4 teaspoon = 4 mL
1 teaspoon = 5 mL
1 tablespoon = 15 mL
2 tablespoons = 30 mL
1/4 cup = 60 mL
1/3 cup = 75 mL
1/2 cup = 125 mL
2/3 cup = 150 mL
3/4 cup = 175 mL
1 cup = 250 mL
2 cups = 1 pint = 500 mL
3 cups = 750 mL
4 cups = 1 quart = 1 L

VOLUME MEASUREMENTS (fluid)

1 fluid ounce (2 tablespoons) = 30 mL
4 fluid ounces (1/2 cup) = 125 mL
8 fluid ounces (1 cup) = 250 mL
12 fluid ounces (1 1/2 cups) = 375 mL
16 fluid ounces (2 cups) = 500 mL

WEIGHTS (mass)

1/2 ounce = 15 g
1 ounce = 30 g
3 ounces = 90 g
4 ounces = 120 g
8 ounces = 225 g
10 ounces = 285 g
12 ounces = 360 g
16 ounces = 1 pound = 450 g

DIMENSIONS

1/16 inch = 2 mm
1/8 inch = 3 mm
1/4 inch = 6 mm
1/2 inch = 1.5 cm
3/4 inch = 2 cm
1 inch = 2.5 cm

OVEN TEMPERATURES

250°F = 120°C
275°F = 140°C
300°F = 150°C
325°F = 160°C
350°F = 180°C
375°F = 190°C
400°F = 200°C
425°F = 220°C
450°F = 230°C

BAKING PAN SIZES

Utensil	Size in Inches/Quarts	Metric Volume	Size in Centimeters
Baking or Cake Pan (square or rectangular)	8×8×2	2 L	20×20×5
	9×9×2	2.5 L	23×23×5
	12×8×2	3 L	30×20×5
	13×9×2	3.5 L	33×23×5
Loaf Pan	8×4×3	1.5 L	20×10×7
	9×5×3	2 L	23×13×7
Round Layer Cake Pan	8×1½	1.2 L	20×4
	9×1½	1.5 L	23×4
Pie Plate	8×1¼	750 mL	20×3
	9×1¼	1 L	23×3
Baking Dish or Casserole	1 quart	1 L	—
	1½ quart	1.5 L	—
	2 quart	2 L	—